THE WAY WE WERE
THE WAY WE ARE

Volume 2

Vahe H. Apelian

V.H. Apelian
January 2016
Loveland, OH

A Collection of Bilingual Heritage Articles

DEDICATION

To

Samara Marie Apelian,

our granddaughter.

May she grow up in a sound mind and body
and appreciative of her heritages.

PREFACE

This volume is a sequel to the first. There will be a third volume as well that will consist of book reviews and translations.

It is a collection mostly of articles depicting people, events and issues. They are narrated for leisurely and entertaining reading while being informative.

The articles in this volume comprise broader range of subjects and topics while the first volume pertained mostly if not exclusively to Kessab, the Armenian enclave in the in northwestern Syria. Most of the articles in this volume have also appeared in Keghart.com website devoted to community activities, human rights and democracy

This volume is a bilingual. Two in Armenian are my own and the remaining is authored by my mother and pertains to her teaching career that spanned for almost five decades.

Other than the cover pictures, the rest are not captioned as they are easily inferable and pertain to the story with which they are depicted.

Vahe H. Apelian
Loveland, OH

TABLE OF CONTENTS

	Title	Page
1	The Dreamer	1
2	Genius With Words	13
3	Goodell Among the Armenians	23
4	Tale of an Armenian Hymnal	33
5	The Legend of Shake'	39
6	Krikor Guyjikian's Legacy	45
7	Saroyan's Popular But Nonsensical Quote	51
8	Triumphant Israel (Vahan) Pilikian	57
9	Righteous Turks of Erayli	63
10	Wobbling Pillars	69
11	A Memorable Interview	75
12	There Is No Respect	83
13	The Case of Community Nursing Home	89
14	A Rebel With a Cause	97
15	Love in Medz *Yeghern*	103
16	Remembering Simon Simonian	109
17	Shahnour, Doomster of Western Armenian	117
18	An Undisputable Expert	123
19	Siamanto's Dance	129
20	*Vorbes Hishadag Anmoratsoutian*	139
21	#RebuildKessab	149
22	Խաչակիրը	161
23	Սպղանաց Մակար	167
24	Գաբրիէլը Ղափանի Մէջ (Զուարթ Աբէլեան)	177
25	Խմբային Ասմունքներ (Զուարթ Աբէլեան)	183
26	Դէմքեր, Դէպքեր եւ Ցուցեր (Զուարթ Աբէլեան)	187
27	Cover Picture Captions	195

1. The Dreamer

Ի՞նչ փոյթ կեանքը մեռնող

Երբոր երազը կ՚ապրի

Երբոր երազն անմահ է

Դանիէլ Վարուժան

What of the dying life

When the dream lives on

When the dream is immortal

Taniel Varoujan

THE BUDDING POET[1]

The year 2014 marked the 130th anniversary of poet Taniel Varoujan's birth. He was born on April 20, 1884 in a village on the outskirts of Sepastia in Turkey where he had his primary education. He hailed from the Chboukarian family. His father Krikor worked as a broker in Istanbul. His mother Takouhie was a homemaker. They had four sons. Taniel was the eldest. His siblings, all male, were named Vahan, Bedros and Arshag. The youngest was 24 years junior to him and was two-years-old when Varoujan got married.

In 1896, the year of the Hamidian Massacres, he was sent to Istanbul where his father lived, to further his education. He attended the Mekhitarian School and continued his education at Mourad-Rafaelian School in Venice, Italy. In 1906 he started attending the Ghent University in Belgium where he studied literature and economics.

He published his first book of poetry at the age of twenty-one in a periodical that was published in San Lazzaro Island in Venice. It was titled *Սարսուռներ (Sarsourner, i.e Shivers)*. The Hamidian Massacres and the imprisonment of his father had left profound impressions on the budding poet.

THE TEACHER

After the declaration of the Ottoman Constitution in 1909, he returned home and started teaching at the Aramian School of Sepastia until 1912. Some of his students later wrote about him in their memoirs. One of them named Arakel Badreg reminisced that one year, just before their summer break, he and other students visited Varoujan in his paternal house. On their way they passed through the same road and along the same stream that Varoujan mentioned in his autobiography in Teotig's almanac[2]. In it Varoujan had written: "That's where I spent my childhood, under the melancholic shade of the pomegranate trees along the stream, mischievously throwing pebbles to the ducks." As they passed by the same stream one of them remarked to a classmate saying: "you better throw pebbles at the ducks too, perhaps you may become another Varoujan one day".

Varoujan and his parents welcomed them. It was a two-story building, simply furnished. A vegetable garden surrounded the house. The library of the poet was rich with books. Varoujan read a poem by Dante and then asked them, "Did you pay attention to the language's silvery beauty? The Italian is a song; it is a song".

THE POET

Not long after his return from Europe (1909) he published his second literary work, a book of poetry titled *Ձեղին սիրտը (Tseghen Sirde, i.e. The Heart of the Race)*. It is there that Varoujan revealed the eminent poet he was. His writing had reached an unsurpassed mastery of language and of depth and form. He was only 25-years-old when he published the literary masterpiece. A great deal has been written about his poetry. Our greatest literary critic, Hagop Oshagan, after reading *The Heart of the Race* declared that Varoujan is our greatest poet. Varoujan had a special approach to writing. Events from his life inspired him and stirred his imagination. Once Father Ghevont Alishan[3] sent one of his books to Catholicos Mgrdich Khrimian[4] inscribing in it "To the Nation's Father". The Catholicos in turn sent him a boxful of soil from Armenia addressed "To The Patriarch of the Nation". Inspired by the exchanges Varoujan wrote one of his most memorable poems titled *կարմիր հողը (Garmir Hogheh, i.e. The*

Red Soil) that appeared in *The Heart of the Race* collection of poetry.

In 1912 he published his third book of poetry titled *Հեթանոս երգեր (Hetanos Yerker, i.e, Pagan Songs).* Varoujan continued to write even when he was imprisoned at the onset of the Genocide. His last manuscript was saved after his martyrdom by bribing the officials . It was apparent that his last literary work was not complete. Nonetheless it was published posthumously in 1921. The book was titled *Հացին երգը (Hatsen Yerkeh, i.e. The Song of Bread).* The poems celebrate the toiling Armenian peasantry. He describes the peasant standing tall and imposing in the fields he cultivates.

THE POET'S MARRIAGE

To supplement his teacher's meager salary at the Aramian School, Varoujan gave private lessons to a young girl named Araxie (Araksi), the daughter of a wealthy local Armenian family. As was the customs at the time, Araxie had been promised in betrothal to the son of another wealthy family when still in her crib. That's why Araxie's mother always chaperoned her daughter and attended her classes. The improbable happened. The teacher and the student fell madly in love with each other. Rumors started flying in greater Sepastia. The classes ended abruptly and Araxie's parents and the prospective in-laws began hasty preparations for an earlier-than-planned wedding, but Araxie remained adamant refusing to comply with her parent's wishes. Instead of a wealthy husband she preferred the country teacher of meager means. The situation became the talk of the town among the Armenians amd pitted one camp against the other. Many regarded the incident scandalous and blamed the teacher for having seduced his student. Some supported him and wanted the lovers to marry. The animosity toward Taniel Varoujan became so much so that he began carrying a stick to defend himself should he be attacked. Finally the prominent Armenian freedom fighter Sepastatsi Mourad who, as his name indicates, was also from Sepastia intervened in favor of Varoujan. Larger than life stature of the eminent freedom fighter was such that no one would oppose his decision. His ruling quelled all gossip. Three children were born from the young lovers' union: Veronic, Haig and Armen.

THE POET'S DEATH

In April 1915 Varoujan, along with many other Armenian notables, was apprehended in Istanbul. Their arrest would be the prelude of what would be the greatest catastrophe that has befallen on the Armenian nation, the Genocide. He was subjected to torture and died a slow and painful death on August 26 near a Turkish village called Changher. He was 31-years-old.

Varoujan's father was killed in Sepastia. The fates of his mother and two brothers are not known. Only his brother Vahan survived. For many years he worked in a printing shop in Paris.

Varoujan's widow Araxie remarried and emigrated to The United States. As to their children; Haig settled in Fresno, California where he worked for a local newspaper. He passed away in 2002. His other son Armen settled in Hawaii with his family where passed away. His daughter Veronic worked in New York City public libraries. She would always attend the April 24 commemorations and reflect upon her talented father.

THE POET REMEMBERED

In 1958 the Armenian students in Belgium secured the permission of the Ghent University to have the bilingual plaque, depicted above, commemorating Taniel Varourjan literary legacy be placed in the library hall of the university he attended. The unveiling of the memorial plaque took place on February 9, 1958. The poet's widow Mrs. Araxie Varoujan-Apigian attended the unveiling. A representative from ministry of culture; the president of the university; Luc-André Marcel (who had translated Varoujan's work into French); Frédéric Feydit, the eminent Armenian linguist; writer Garo Poladian, and Edouard Emirzian (the latter on behalf of the Armenian students) took part in the ceremony and spoke about the poet. Academician Pierre Maes, a former classmate delivered a most poignant personal testimony about the slain poet. He said that not long after admission Taniel Varoujan mastered the French language well enough to deliver a lecture at the history department about Armenians and Armenian culture. Varoujan would read to him, the academician said, the poems he had written leaving him mesmerized by the eloquence of their sound and delivery, although he did not understand Armenian.

Varoujan's appeal as a prominent poet continues to reverberate to this day. His poetry bears a universal theme cherishing labor and humanity.

Attached is Tatul Sonentz-Papazian's translation of Taniel Varoujan's *Անդաստան (Antastan)*[5] poem.

Notes:

1. This article has drawn extensively from Levon Sharoyan's postings in Aleppo Armenians Facebook Group.

2. Teotig (Teotoros Lapçinciyan) (1873; Constantinople (Istanbul), Ottoman Empire- 1928; Paris, France), was an Armenian writer and publisher known for publishing an almanac titled *Ամէնուն Տարեցոյցը (Amenun Daretsuyts, i.e. Everyone's Almanac)*. It was published annually between 1907 and 1929.

3. Father Ghevont Alishan (1820-1901), also spelled Ghevond Alishan) was an ordained Armenian Catholic priest, historian and a poet. He was a member of the Mkhitarist Congregation in Venice since 1838. He is credited to have the designed the Armenian tri-color flag of today.

4. Mkrtich Khrimian (April 4, 1820 - October 27, 1907)

was an Armenian religious and political leader. He served as the Armenian Patriarch of Constantinople (1869-1873), as the Prelate of Van (1880-1885) and was elected as Catholicos of All Armenian (1892-1907). He is known more by his endearing moniker as *Khrimian Hayrik.* Hayrik is an affectionate term for father.

5. There is no English word for *Antastan* to my knowledge. It means a vast expanse.

Անդաստան

Դանիէլ Վարուժան

Antastan

Taniel Varoujan

Արեւելեան կողմն աշխարհի
Խաղաղութի՜ւն թող ըլլայ...
Ո՛չ արիւններ, քրտինք հոսին
Լայն երակին մէջ ակօսին.
Ու երբ հնչէ կոչնակն ամէն գիւղակի՛
Օրհներգութ՜իւն թող ըլլայ:

At the Eastern part of the earth
Let there be peace...
Let sweat, not blood, flow
In the broad vein of the furrow,
And at the toll of each hamlet's bell
Let there rise hymns of exaltation.

Արեւմտեան կողմն աշխարհի
Բերրիութի՜ւն թող ըլլայ...
Ամէն աստղ գող կայլակի,
Ու ամէն հասկ ցուլէ ոսկի.
Եւ ոչխարներն երբ սարին վրայ արածին՛
Մ'իլ ու ծաղիկ թող ըլլայ:

At the Western part of the earth
Let there be fecundity ...
Let each star sparkle with dew,
And each husk be cast in gold,
And as the sheep graze on the hills
Let bud and blossom bloom.

Հիւսիսային կողն աշխարհի
Առատութի՜ւն թող ըլլայ...
Ոսկի ծովուն մէջ ցորեանին
Յաւէտ լողայ թող գերանդին.
Ու լայն ամբարն ադուննեռուն երբ բացուի՛
Բերկրութիւն թող ըլլայ:

At the Northern part of the earth
Let there be abundance ...
In the golden sea of the wheat field
Let the scythe swim incessantly
And as gates of granaries open wide
Jubilation let there be.

Հարաւային կողմն աշխարհի

At the Southern part of the earth

11

Պտղաբերում բող ըլլայ...

Մադկի՛ մեղրը փեթակնըրուն,

Ցորդի գինին բաժակնըրուն

Ու երբ թխեն հարսերը հացը բարի

Սիրերգութի՛ւն բող ըլլայ:

Let all things bear fruit...

Let the honey thrive in the beehive

And may the wine run over the cups

And when brides bake the blessed
bread

Let the sound of song rise and
spread.

2. Genius With Words

The Armenian Apostolic Church commemorates the sacred feast of *Սուրբ Յակոբ (Sourp Hagop, i.e. Saint Hagop)[1]* on the Saturday of the second week of December. On that weekend, customarily people visit, congratulate and wish well family members, relatives, friends and acquaintances named Hagop.

There are many notable lay individuals named Hagop and among them prominently stands out Hagop Martayan, also known as Agop Dilaçar[2]. He was an eminent linguist and one of the main architects of the modern written Turkish language. He was born in 1895 in Istanbul and graduated from the local Robert College in 1915 where he was appointed English language lecturer and later lectured at the Sofia University, Bulgaria specializing in Ottoman Turkish and ancient Eastern languages. He was proficient in many other languages as well.

Turkish used to be written with a version of Arabic scripts. As part of his efforts to modernize Turkey, the founder and the first president of the Turkish Republic Mustafa Kamal Atatürk issued a decree to have the Arabic based script replaced with a Latin character based alphabet. Martayan's reputation as an expert linguist was so widely known that Atatürk personally invited him to attend the First Turkish Language Congress on Sept. 22, 1932. Atatürk presided over the congress. Martayan accepted the invitation and from that point until his death he devoted his life to the Turkish language.

Atatürk remained so impressed by Hagop Martayan's linguistic expertise that he suggested the surname Dilaçar for him when the Law on Family Names came into effect in 1934. Dilaçar means someone who opens a new language. Hagop accepted the name and henceforth in Turkish circles he became known as Agop Dilaçar. However, he did not drop his baptismal family name altogether but used it signing his articles in Armenian.

From 1936 to 1952, he taught history and language at the Ankara University. He was appointed editor-in-chief (1942-1960) of the Turkish Encyclopedia. He was also the main advisor and the secretary-general of the newly formed Turkish Language Assocition. A position he held continuing his research in linguistics until his death on 12 September 1979, in Istanbul.

Hagop Martayan-Dilaçar lived in Ankara but continued to maintain his ties with the Istanbul Armenian community. In the '50s he often contributed articles to the Istanbul-based *Մարմարա* (*Marmara*)[3] Armenian newspaper glorifying important Armenian historical events. He declared 1951, the 1,500 anniversary of the Vartanian War, *Սուրբ Տարի (Sourp Dari, i.e Holy Year).* On that occasion he wrote many articles in the newspaper about the protracted war between Armenia and Persia and had it published as a booklet.

To have a better perspective of the scope and breath of his knowledge of Armenian literature it's worth noting the titles of some of the articles he wrote in *Marmara* in that period: *Հանդէս Ամսօրեայ-ի 80-ամեակը (The 80th Anniversary of Hantes Amsoria)[4]; 400-ամեակ պոլսահայ տպագրութեան (The 400th Anniversary of Armenian Printing in Istanbul); Մեր առաջին համալսարանները (Our First Universities); Հայերէնը դարերէն ի վար (The Armenian Through Centuries); Մեր արեւմտահայերէն* (Our Western Armenian); *Ճանչել* *զիմաստութիւն եւ զխրատ* (To Know Wisdom and Instruction); and many, many more.

Martayan-Dilaçar made his deep appreciation and love of the Armenian language and literature amply evident in the early 1960s when he started publishing in *Marmara* articles under the general header *Համայնապատկեր հայ մշակոյթի* (A *Panoramic View of Armenian Culture)*. It was an extensive and in-depth study that appeared daily in the newspaper consecutively for many years, for some 1,500 days. This exhaustive study was assembled and published in three

volumes after his death. Those who have perused these volumes remain at awe of his encyclopedic knowledge of Armenian culture.

Rober Haddedjian[4], playwright and the long-time editor-in-chief of *Marmara*, was a confidant and friend of the eminent linguist. He bears witness to Hagop Martayan-

Dilaçar and his wife's love of Armenian culture. The eminent linguist and his wife Meline' lived in Ankara isolated from the

Armenian community. They felt a strong need to associate with Armenians and speak the language. They sent their son Vahe to Istanbul to attend the Mekhitarian School to receive an Armenian education and to continue to maintain his ties with his people. In the 1960s Hagop Martayan-Dilaçar often visited Istanbul and liked to meet young Armenian writers who would remain mesmerized by his encyclopedic knowledge

When Haddedjian visited them in Ankara for the very first time he was in awe of his massive library of thousands of volumes, encyclopedias and dictionaries. He was a living encyclopedia himself, a modern-day living computer where by pressing a button one would get encyclopedic information with figures and dates.

Last but not the least, Hagop was very proud of his baptismal name. He had a palm-size notebook where on each page he inscribed his name in the native characters of many languages, dead or living. Haddedjian said that with that booklet he paid homage to his parents and his baptismal name and made amply evident of his encyclopedic knowledge of languages living and dead. According to Wikipedia he was proficient in 22 languages, and in addition to Armenian and Turkish, he knew English, Greek, Spanish, Azerbaijani, Latin, German Russian and Bulgarian. He called his booklet ՅԱԿՈԲԱՊԱՏՈՒՄ (*Hagopabadoum*), sort of *Hagopedia.*

In spite of his contributions to the modern Turkish language and to the Armenian culture, a small but vocal group of Turks and Armenians despised him. He seemed to have been caught in the middle and aroused the suspicions of both parties.

First the Turks: As the editor-in-chief of the Turkish Encyclopedia, Martayan-Dilaçar wrote countless entries. When it came to the letter E, he wrote about the Armenians under *Ermenlir* (Armenian in Turkish) header as any objective academician would have done. However, the government-appointed censors refused to include it in the encyclopedia. Instead they delegated someone else with the task of preparing the entry about Armenians. Martayan-Dilaçar took offense and regarded it a personal affront, a treacherous deed. He was greatly saddened.

The Armenians: When he was publishing his exhaustive study of the Armenian culture in Marmara in the 1960s, another Armenian newspaper in Istanbul, ժամանակ *(Jamanag, i.e. Time),* engaged with him over an obscure academic debate as to whether the Armenian word կապարիչ *(gaparitch),* that customariy means lid. Martayan-Dilaçar had used the word for cover of a book, instead of the commonly used Armenian word for it, կողք *(go'ghk)*. In spite of all the evidence the linguist produced to justify its use, his opponent continued his relentless objection and turned it into a personal attack. The episode so angered and outraged him that he stopped contributing to Marmara and ceased writing in Armenian.

He passed away in Istanbul on September 12, 1979. He is buried in the pantheon of the Armenian intellectuals and artists in the Armenian cemetery of Istanbul.[5]

Note:

1. The feast is dedicated to the memory of St. Jacob (James) of Nisibis who was one of the signatories in the First Council of Niceae in 325.

2. This article has drawn extensively from Levon Sharoyan's postings in Aleppo Armenians Facebook Group.

3. *Marmara* (*Մարմարա*) is an Armenian-language daily newspaper in publication since August 1940 in Istanbul. Its editor is Robert Haddedjian.

4. Rober Haddeciyan (also spelled and pronounced as Haddedjian) (Ռոպէր Հատտէճեան) (born 1926) in Istanbul and also known as Rober Haddeler, is a writer, playwright, and since 1967 editor-in-chief of Marmara.

5. Hrach Kalsahakian pictured Hagop Martayan-Dilaçar's gravesite during a visit to Istanbul. He posted it in Aleppo Armenians Facebook Group. He wrote: "The picture is from Shishli (Şişli in Turkish) Armenian Cemetery, the main cemetery of the Armenians on the European side of Istanbul. As an Armenian, he had no other place to be buried. The tomb is part of Pantheon of Intellectuals and Artists, (Պանթէոն Մատուրականներու եւ Արուեստագէտներու)."
It's worth noting that the other Armenian cemetery of

Istanbul, the Pangaltı Armenian Cemetery, originally belonged to the Sourp Hagop Armenian Church, was demolished in the '30s and replaced by big hotels and the Taksim Gezi Park where demonstrators took place in 2013 to protect the park from developers.

VOLUME 2

3. Goodell Among the Armenians

During family discussions in my formative years, I would hear the elders of the family say that the American missionaries failing to evangelize a single Muslim Turk resorted to evangelizing the Christian Armenian subjects of the Ottoman Empire in Turkey.

My impressions changed when I read the memoirs of Rev. William Goodell who played a prominent role in establishing the Protestant community in the Ottoman Empire. The book is titled *Forty*

Years in the Turkish Empire or Memoirs of Rev. William Goodell D.D, Late Missionary of A.B.C.F.M at Constantinople. His son-in-law, E. D. G. Prime has edited the memoir. It was published by Robert Carter and Brothers (New York). Its fifth edition is posted on line by Google and is dated 1878. The quotes in this article are from the on-line book.

Rev. William Goodell left the United States and embarked on his overseas mission in 1822. After a long sojourn in Malta, Lebanon, and Syria, he arrived to Constantinople, as Istanbul was known then. He had embarked on his mission on behalf of the American Board of Commissioners for Foreign Missions (A.B.C.F.M.), the first U.S. missionary organization.

I was surprised to read that Rev. Goodell's primary, if not sole, mission was evangelizing the Armenians. I quote "When Mr. Goodell went to Constantinople, his mission was to the Armenians". Mr. Goodell was entrusted with the mission to Turkey proper because of his knowledge of

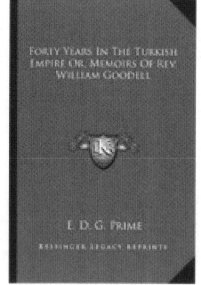

Armenian and Turkish he had mastered while in Malta, Syria and Lebanon. He was also fluent in Arabic, Greek and Italian. He translated the Bible into "Armeno-Turkish", that is to say a Bible that reads Turkish but is in Armenian characters. It was a twenty years long endeavor.

This assertion was a revelation to me but it made sense. Sultan's Sublime Porte would have never allowed American missionaries free rein to evangelize Turks. It caved in to the Western powers and allowed Americans missionaries in the Ottoman Empire as long as their evangelism was carried among its Christian subjects. In all probability the missionaries and their organizations, if not also their governments, were warmed of dire consequences should they attempt evangelize Turks. No wonder then not a single Muslim Turk was evangelized.

Why would A.B.C.F.M embark on its mission, I wondered, singling Armenians when there were other Christian minorities in the empire, such as Greeks and Assyrians? Reading the memoirs presented an interesting picture of a way of the Armenian community's life in the Empire that did not have a natural evolution for reasons we all know all too well.

Rev. William Goodell arrived in Constantinople on June 9, 1831. In a letter to a friend in the United States, he noted:

"My family is said to be the first who has ever visited this place."

Constantinople, where the Goodells established their residency, presented the following demographics. I quote: "The city of Constantinople contained, including the suburbs, a population of about 1,000,000 of various nationalities and religions. The Turks and other Mohammedans comprised more than half; the Greeks and Armenians each numbered 150,000, the former being the more numerous, there were about 50,000 Jews; the remainder was made of Franks and people from almost every part of the world". Istanbul's demographic constituency was much different than it is now and the change did not come about through natural evolution.

These distinct ethnic communities naturally intermingled but "for the most part occupied different quarters of the city with the Turks having almost exclusive possession of the city proper."

The Millet System that constituted the core of the Ottoman Empire governance appeared odd to this visiting American missionary who found it to be an "anomalous form of government, the Sublime Porte, as the Sultan's government is called, being supreme, while each separate nation has its own head." In the case of the Armenians it was the Patriarch of Constantinople who was also the civil head of the Armenian community (Millet)[1].

The A.B.C.F.M. board and Rev. Goodell knew well that the Armenians 'were descendents of the ancient inhabitants of Armenia. The nation embraced Christianity about the commencement of the fourth century". The zealous missionary and the organization that supported his mission apparently had already determined, even before the missionary arrived into the fold of the Armenians in the Ottoman Empire, that the Armenian Church needed to embrace the "truth". According to Rev. Goodell, the Armenian (Apostolic) Church 'has almost wholly given up to superstition and to idolatrous worship of saints, including Virgin Mary, pictures, etc. "

There appears to be a more pragmatic and practical, if not a strategic reason as well, for A.B.C.F.M and Rev. Goodell to single out the Armenians for their mission. I quote: "The Armenians were an enterprising people, and the great wealth of the bankers, who were nearly all Armenians, made them very influential throughout the empire, even with the Turkish officials, who were largely dependent upon them for pecuniary advances and assistance. The various connections of this people with different parts of the country, and the influence which they were in a position to exert, in promoting the spread of the Gospel in Turkey, made it exceedingly desirable that they should embrace the truth. "

Mr. Goodell's arrival in Constantinople coincided with a reformation movement within the Armenian Apostolic Church. Fifteen years later, and after much agony and ecstasy, on July 1, 1846, 'Forty persons, of whom three were women, voluntarily entered onto covenant with God and with each other, and we, in the name of all the evangelical churches of Christendom, rose and formally recognized and acknowledged them as a true church of Christ." The assembly on that day became the foundation of The Armenian Evangelical Church. Its adherents would continue to render much service to the Armenian nation enriching it way more than one would have expected from the meager demographic constituency of its faithful.

Image © ArmenianHouse.org

On November 15, 1847, 'the grand vizier issued a firman, declaring that the Christian subjects of the Ottoman government professing Protestantism should constitute a separate community...This firman was so worded that converts form among the Greeks and Jews who joined the Protestants might enjoy the same immunities." The firman makes obvious by omission that Muslim Turks joining would not be recognized as a member of the new religious community, that of the newly established Protestant Millet. On November 27, 1850 Sultan Abdul Mejid ratified the edict that became the "Magna Carta" of the Protestant community that stands to this day in the Middle East. The Armenian Evangelicals are part and parcel of the Protestant Community.

Having lived through this turbulent period for over the 30 years, Rev. Goodell left Constantinople on June 27, 1865 some 40 years after leaving his homeland. Through those over four decades, he had visited his country only once. Before taking leave for good, he addressed his brethren in the Evangelical Churches in Turkey and wrote saying: "When we first came among you, your were not a distinct people, nor did we expect you ever would be; for we had not sectarian object in view, it being no part of our plan to meddle with ecclesiastical affairs. Our sole desire was to preach Christ and Him crucified."

When Rev. Goodell took his leave and left for home, the Armenian Evangelical Church was firmly entrenched among the Armenians. That became the last major schism within the Armenian Apostolic Church, the first being the establishment of the Armenian Catholic Church by Pope Benedict XIV In 1749. Up to that point the only Church for Armenians was their Apostolic Church. It was established when the Armenians accepted Christianity by the order of their Kind Trdat in 301 AD. The church anointed a newborn with Holy *Muron*[2]. No person would have have been accepted as an Armenian without having been anointed with it.

After his return to the United States, Rev. Goodell visited friends and gave sermons. He lived with son and namesake in Philadelphia where he passed away on Feb. 16, 1867.

Note

1. The millet system was a separate legal governance of a confessional community within the Ottoman Empire, such as Armenian Apostolic Christians, allowing it to govern itself under its own rules.

2. The holy anointing oil of the Armenian Apostolic Church is called the Holy Muron. It is composed of olive oil and other aromas and flowers. The remaining portion of the previous blessed holy oil is poured into the newly prepared oil during the blessing ceremony. It is said that this very procedure has been followed since the Armenians accepted Christianity as their national religion in 301 AD. Portions from blessed Holy Muron are then distributed to all of the Armenian churches throughout the world.

4. Tale of an Armenian Hymnal

Several years ago I purchased an Armenian hymnal on eBay from a bookseller in Turkey. It is titled Հայուն Երգարանը *(Hayoun Yerkaraneh, i.e The Armenian's Hymnal).* It had been compiled by Hmayag Aramiants. The hardcover hymnal was printed in Istanbul in 1911. Its 318 pages are very well preserved. There is a signature on the inner page that is hard to decipher to ascertain the name of the person who, in all probability, owned the hymnal at one time.

The hymnal is dedicated to the legendary Armenian woman named Shake' who hurled herself down a precipice in Sassoon lest she be abducted by a Turk or a Kurd. There is a drawing of her with a rifle on her shoulder and a child in her lap looking down the precipice. The following is inscribed as its caption: "Shake', The Immortal Heroine of Sassoun".

The dedication reads in part as follows: "Adorable Shake', you illuminated a page of our modern day history with your heroism and you elevated the honor of the Armenian Woman and of the Armenian Race. Forgive me to dedicate this modest work in your memory as a token of my deep admiration towards you and to your innocent child."

The hymnal leans towards international brotherhood, the cornerstone of socialism. There is a picture of Karl Max along an Armenian song titled Յեղափոխութիւն *(Heghapokhoutiun, i.e Revolution).* There are Armenian songs dedicated to the social brotherhood, such as titled *Proletariat* (in Armenian characters); *Enger Panvor* (*Comrade Laborer*); *International* (in Latin characters). The hymnal also contains at least one Turkish song tiled *Ittihad Marshe* (*The March of the Ittihad*) in Armenian characters reading Turkish. The eminent musicologist Bedros Alahaidoyan claims that the few pictures of the non-Armenians in the hymnal are that of noted European socialists.

The hymnal is full of pictures as attested by Hmayag Aramiants, the compiler of the popular songs of the era. Most of the pictures are of Armenian freedom fighters - *fedayens-* some of whom are armed. There is a full-page picture of a poster of two armed freedom fighters displaying a flag that reads *Mah gam Azadoutiun* (*Freedom or Death*).

All these *fedayens* pitted themselves against oppression. The arms they carried in the pictures were directed against the Hamidian regime, nontheless Turkish regime. Many if not most of the songs are in praise of their bravery. How is it, I thought, Hmayag Aramiants mustered the courage to publish such a hymnal in Istanbul in 1911? The answer is in its introduction whose naïveté caught my attention.

The Armenians of Constantinople celebrated the Ottoman constitution of 1908 and the establishment of the government led by the Committee of Union and Progress with unprecedented zeal. Posters appeared in Armenian and Ottoman Turkish languages proclaiming the dawn of the new era for "Liberty, Equality, and Justice". The euphoria for the new social order seems to have blinded the Armenian community in Istanbul. Apparently even the 1909 Adana Massacre that was not confined Adana only but spread to the other cities of the historical Armenian Cilicia and to northern Syria did not seem to have awakened the Armenian subjects in the capital of the Ottoman Empire or dampened the spirits and the optimism of Hmayag Aramiants for the promise of the impending social changes for the more liberal, equal and just larger society within the Empire.

In the introduction, Hmayag Aramiants, trusting the "new order" of "Liberty, Equality, Justice", naively noted that the Armenians living under the Hamidian regime could not have possibly chosen any other path towards social justice and could not have adopted a political alignment other than that manifested by the Armenian resistance against the oppressive state. The popular songs he had compiled were in the praise of these revolutionaries. Furthermore, he noted, the self-preservation efforts of the Armenians under Hamid's Armenocidal policies are in fact no more than manifestations of noble and obedient citizenship that were eventually manifested "on the flag dedicated to Liberty, Equality and Justice". Therefore, Hmayag concludes that "the just manifest of rightful Anger and Racial Self-Determination against the oppressive regime cannot disturb the spiritual tranquility of free citizens, be they government employees, be they servants of laws or just citizens".

I do not think I need to elaborate on the sinister plan that was being laid down as Hmayag euphorically swayed by the promise of impending change was writing the introductory notes of the hymnal. The naïveté of Hmayag and the majority of the Armenians in opening themselves to their inner most humane needs, I believe, played in the hands of those who were planning the "final solution" and served to justify the "righteousness" of their cause. That is not to say that the absence of such overt humane outbursts by the Armenian subjects would have changed the hearts and the minds of the new masters of the Ottoman Empire and set aside their policy of "cleansing" the Empire's "heartland ".

With regard to the Armenians, especially their leadership, including the flamboyant intellect, lawyer and member of the Ottoman Parliament Krikor Zohrab; it would have been humanly impossible for them to imagine that extermination of such a magnitude, we have come to term as Genocide since 1943, could have possibly be fathomed and planned for execution by other human beings, be it Turks.

Over the years I have perused the hymnal many a time and wondered what happened to Hmayag Aramiants four years after publishing his hymnal. In his introduction he promises, if circumstances permit he writes, to publish a second volume of the hymnal to complete the compiling of the Armenian revolutionary and nationalistic songs that were not included in this volume. Did he survive? I do not know of any other hymnal from Hmayag Aramiants.

5. The Legend of Shaké

The black and white pencil drawing of Shaké, with a rifle on her shoulder and a child in her lap looking down a precipice in the mountains of Sassoun (Sasun), is rather a familiar drawing. Sassoun is a region in the rugged mountain country southwest of Lake Van historically populated by Armenians. It has given rise to the Armenian national epic called Սասնա ծռեր *(Sasna tsřer, i.e. Daredevils of Sassoun)* whose main hero is Սասունցի Դավիթ *(Sasuntsi Davit, i.e. David of Sassoun).*

I had always assumed that Shake' is a mythical figure, much like David of Sassoun. I recently found out that it is not the case. She was flesh and blood. Her story was depicted in May 29, 2011 issue of in the Armenian weekly *Nor Gyank* written by Rosa Pashinian who is a candidate for doctoral degree in history in Armenia.

Here is an abridged summary of the article she wrote.

'On July 15, 1894, in the house of Krikor (Krko) Mosseyan, the chieftain of Sheneg, the princes of Sassoun gathered to discuss how to defend themselves against the expected onslaught. Women were also present at the gathering. Notable among them was Shaké Mosseyan, the wife of Krko's elder brother. She was noted for her bravery and for her outspokenness.

Hampartsoum Boyajian, a former medical student in Constantinople, who was better known by his nom-de-guerre Murat, addressed them saying that the enemy forces have encircled Sassoun and war is inevitable. He exhorted them to fight to their last drop of blood to defend their mountains and the sanctity of their households.

The authorities were not only demanding that Sassountsis pay 175 thousand silver gurush to cover their alleged taxes over the past seven years, but were also demanding that the 67 notables of Dalvoreg of Sassoun and the clergy present themselves in Moush to show their obedience. Furthermore all those in Sassoun from elsewhere were ordered to present themselves to the authorities. The aim of the Ottoman High Porte was to decapitate Sassoun of its leadership and subsequently subjugate, if not massacre the people. The enemy forces were assembled in Moush. Kurdish and Turkish irregulars had also joined. The combined forces far outnumbered the people of Sassoun.

On July 28, 1894 the villagers of Sheneg engaged fighting the Kurds and the regular forces. The Sassountsis from the village Semal joined force and succeeded in pushing back the onslaught. The women of Sassoun, led by Shaké Mosseyan, helped the fighters by providing food and distributing ammunition. The fighting continued until August 23. The enemy supplemented the fight with fresh forces, while the Sassountsi fighters, running out of ammunition and food, retreated. At one point Krko Mosseyan and his men left the defense of the mountain to the women of Sassoun and ventured out to secure food and ammunition.

The enemy continued its onslaught and demanded that the women surrender. Realizing that they cannot anymore defend themselves, Shaké, carrying her six-month old child, retreated to the edge of a precipice and told the women that it is either surrender to the enemy or die. She then hurled herself with her child into the abyss."

Sasun: Villagers of Semal

The bravery of the women of Sassoun during combat is sung in a popular nationalistic song that has survived to this day. Songs were dedicated to Murat as well. Dr. Antranig Chalabian picked Murat as one of the seven great Armenian freedom fighters in his book titled "Revolutionary Figures". Murat was referred to as *Metz Murat*, i.e. Murat the Great to distinguish him from the other legendary freedom fighter Murat of Sebastia.

A legend about the feat of Shaké was also born. The legend must have been so poignant at one time that an unknown artist depicted her image in a penciled drawing of a woman at the edge of a precipice with a rifle hanging on her shoulder and her child in her lap. There does not seem to be any record as to the whereabout of the original drawing. Hmayag Aramiants dedicated the hymnal he published in Constantinople in 1911 in her memory and included a copy of the drawing in his dedication.

After the fall of Sassoun, the surviving Sassountsis were driven from their mountains into the flatlands of Syria where they made their mark. To eke out a living, the once fiercely independent Armenian mountaineers became famous for the bakeries they ran in Aleppo, as the late Simon Simonian, himself of Sassountsi descent, described in his writings. A new legend of sorts was thus born and continues to this day to this day that Sassountsis run the best Armenian bakeries.

VOLUME 2

6. Krikor Gayjikian's Legacy

KRIKOR GAYJIKIAN

As of April 2014, forty-two (42) States have recognized the Armenian Genocide by legislation or by proclamation. Even if the remaining eight States recognize as well, we still will need the recognition by the United States Congress to have the country acknowledge the first genocide of modern history.

I am sure that each State had its own select group of people who strived to secure the recognition. As in most, if not all, endeavors there is "the first among the equals" who drives such grassroots efforts. The case was no different with Ohio, the Buckeye State, nicknamed after the trees that were predominant in the State at one time.

On April 17, 2007, Governor Ted Strickland (D-OH) issued a proclamation recognizing the Armenian Genocide. Shortly after becoming the 40th US State to do so, Mayors Michael Coleman of Cincinnati, Mark Mallory of Columbus and Frank Jackson of Cleveland, issued proclamations in its remembrance.

There is truth, understandably not absolute, in the saying that all politics is local. Ohio is generally recognized to be a swing State in national elections but there is no sizable Armenian community to make a dent in the electoral fates of the candidates. There had to be more than election consideration to have the  Governor of the State and the mayors of its three largest cities issue such proclamations. The person who brought this to fruition is a former congressional candidate, David Krikorian.

David went to Washington, DC and visited the Ohio Congressional delegation advocating passage of the Armenian Genocide legislation. He also called upon his fellow "O-Hye-Oian"s, as he called them, through the many emails he sent to the Armenian denizens of the state asking for their help by soliciting the support of their local elected officials to support his efforts. I am sure many or most did. However, I do not think any of one was more helpful to him than the long interred Krikor Gayjikian.

Who is Krikor Gayjikian?

During his efforts to have Ohio recognize the Genocide, David happened to be in an old-books store in Oakley, which may be considered a yuppie town in greater Cincinnati. There he found a book titled *Martyred Armenia and the Story of My Life* written by Krikor Gayjikian who was born in Gaban in Anatolia and survived the 1894-1896 Hamidian Massacres as a result of which he was orphaned at an early age. Krikor managed to arrive to Cincinnati in 1911. He had a cousin named Boghossian who owned and operated a candy store in the town.

Krikor's book recounted his survival, his experiences in America and a chronology of the Genocide. The book was printed in 1920 by God's Revivalist Press which is affiliated with the over 100 years old God's Bible School in Cincinnati. M.G. Standley of God's Bible School, wrote the foreword on May 17, 1920. Ohio thus unquestionably had welcomed in its midst a survivor of the massacres of the Armenians. He did not speak English and was not familiar with the American way of life when he found refuge in the country. Obviously Ohio gave him all the opportunities to thrive, learn the language and become proficient enough to write the book and have it published in Cincinnati with local support.

The book was a revelation to David Krikorian. Soon he supplemented his drive to the elected officials with electronic copies of the book. The rest is another chapter of our long grassroots quest to have The United States recognize the Genocide of the Armenians.

MARTYRED ARMENIA AND THE STORY OF MY LIFE

As to Krikor Gayjikian, his grand daughter Cindi Helton-Campbell provided the following personal information about her maternal grandfather. After settling down in Cincinnati, he married Osanna Garboushian through an arranged marriage. Osanna was born on March 10, 1892 in Kessab and was a teacher there. Her father's name was Gabriel. Her mother was from the Arslanian family of Kessab. On May 2, 1921 she arrived to Cincinnati where they met for the very frist time and married three days later. The Gayjikians raised four children, Sam, John, Lucy and Rose, Cindi's mother.

Krikor Gayjikian's calling was in mission work. He was a life-long missionary for God's Bible School. From 1929 to 1938 Krikor accompanied by his wife and their three children engaged in mission work in Antioch, Kessab, and in Beirut where their daughter Lucy was born. Upon their return Krikor continued his mission work in down town Cincinnati, OH where he also owned a thrift shop in the later years of his life.

Krikor wrote two additional books as well, titled *A Life Full of Miracles* and *Twentieth Century Miracles*.

Martyred Armenia and the Story of My Life is 308 pages long and is posted on line and can be tracked down through one of the Internet search engines. The book makes for an interesting and inspiring reading.

7. Saroyan's Popular But Nonsensical Quote

"I should like to see any power of the world destroy this race, this small tribe of unimportant people, whose wars have all been fought and lost, whose structures have crumbled, literature is unread, music is unheard, and prayers are no more answered. Go ahead, destroy Armenia. See if you can do it. Send them into the desert without bread or water. Burn their homes and churches. Then see if they will not laugh, sing and pray again. For when two of them meet anywhere in the world, see if they will not create a New Armenia."

I bet most English-speaking Armenians have read William Saroyan's quote. Some may have also bought an inscription of the quote on a plaque. I was no exception. In fact I ordered the larger size and hung it on a wall in our house. Saroyan looms larger than life, especially for Armenians. He was a bear of man with an oversized and impressive mustache. I had the opportunity of meeting him in person when the Armenian community of Beirut lavished upon him a heartfelt warm welcome during the late 1960's or early 1970's. The inhabitants of the Armenian village of Anjar in Lebanon slaughtered lamb as he entered the village. A large entourgage accompanied and escorted him with Musa Dagh traditional davul and zurna. His mustachoed image and his embracing radiant personality remain etched in my memory.

Obviously I had found the quote impressionable otherwise I would not have done what I did. I would read the quote every now and then with some sense of comfort that our growing sons may read it too and over time establish some understanding as to who we are and where do we come from. Over time I established a familiarity with it. When novelty gives way to familiarity, so do feelings give way to reason of varying degree. It is then that it occurred to me to ask myself: "What is this quote really saying?"

First and foremost I saw a pervasive paranoia in the quote: "I should see any power destroy this race". "Go ahead, destroy Armenia, etc. etc. etc". Surely we have had and have our share of enemies but I bet more people on this planet do not know us to ever bother to think of harming us.

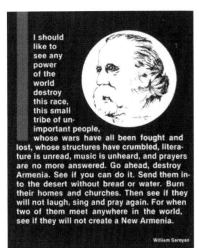

I should like to see any power of the world destroy this race, this small tribe of unimportant people, whose wars have all been fought and lost, whose structures have crumbled, literature is unread, music is unheard, and prayers are no more answered. Go ahead, destroy Armenia. See if you can do it. Send them into the desert without bread or water. Burn their homes and churches. Then see if they will not laugh, sing and pray again. For when two of them meet anywhere in the world, see if they will not create a New Armenia.

William Saroyan

Destroy, but who?

Destroy "this small tribe of unimportant people". Is that what we are? Is this what I want our children to read growing up...that we come from "a tribe of unimportant people"? How would my son's teacher and friends react, I thought, if my son took the plaque to school for a morning class show-and-tell? I felt aghast.

On further thought, I realized that there is more in the quote that kills the spirit than uplifts it. After all we are speaking of a people "whose structures have crumbled, literature is unread, music is unheard, and prayers are no more answered". Gosh, imagine trying to explain this to a child you are raising to be proud of his or her ethnic heritage.

Granted that there are affirmative statements in the quote about Armenians coming together, laughing, singing and creating a new Armenia. All that is good and well but offers little solace after all the paranoia, doom and gloom.

Eventually it occurred to me that the plaque did not cite the source of the quote. Internet search-engines were of no help. I started having doubts whether Saroyan had really said it.

Sometime later I came across a discussion in an Armenian media alleging that Saroyan's quote is a sanitized version of his utterance. The writer said that Saroyan started it with an obscene expression. If I were to use it in an article, more likely than not, editors will censor it. The commentator said that the original quote contains the word 'mother' but not as in the "Holy Mother of God" expression. It would not surprise me that Saroyan would use a foul expression. As I said, he loomed larger than life and had his way when it came to words.

I still don't know for sure if a foul expression precedes the quote. However, it makes more sense to me that it does. Saroyan, more likely than not, said what he said in rage. We are not supposed to sound rational when angry. Our rage is an outlet to express our frustration more so than to make sense. Surely what we say in our rage in not meant to be educational.

For all those who would like to display the quote in their homes, I suggest them to have it inscribed in verbatim and indicate the source once they find it. It's the right thing to do. After all, words, even foul expressions, make sense and may even sound less offensive if they are used in context. Otherwise one may consider doing what I did with its sanitized version, I tucked it away.

VOLUME 2

8. Triumphant Israel (Vahan) Pilikian

One does not need to be a psychiatrist or psychologist or a clairvoyant to affirm that the survivors of the Genocide of the Armenians were traumatized. Modern medicine has coined a name for it, Post-Traumatic Stress Disorder (PTSD).

In North America the acronym is mostly referred to in conjunction with the returning soldiers who had their 'boots on the ground' in foreign 'theaters". The military has its ways of making things palatable through euphemism, doesn't it? These soldiers have all sorts of trained specialists to help them overcome the effects of their traumatic experiences. The survivors of the Armenian Genocide were much less fortunate. They had no such intervention nor could they dream of such interventions. They were left to their lots.

The survivors, however, created their own ways of coping with their traumatic experiences. They helped each other in the makeshift camps and laid the foundation of the modern, prosperous and ever more confidant Armenian Diaspora.

They also resorted to writing. Pen, pencil and paper became their catharsis. In doing so, they created the post-Genocide Armenian literature. Some of them attained the pinnacle of literature (e.g. Antranig Dzarougian). Some created novels that will remain classics of the Western Armenian literature (e.g. Shahan Shahnour). Some had fictitious characters portray themselves and others they knew. Some recounted their experiences as memoirs (e.g. Mushegh Ishkhan, Karnig Panian, and Armen Anoush). Some attained recognition posthumously and only after their memoirs became known to a wider readership, thanks to translation, such as Grigoris Balakian's memoir titled *Armenian Golgotha*.

The memoirs of most of the others remain dormant. Their memoirs first and foremost unburdened them from their trauma. They also penned to pass a legacy to their children. Among such memoirs is the memoir of Israel (Vahan) Pilikian, the father of the gifted and eminent Pilikian brothers in London, Professors Hovhannes and Khachatur.

The Pilikian name was not unfamiliar in the close-knit Armenian community of Beirut. I knew of the name even before my teens. A family relative worked as a pharmacy technician at the Pilikian Pharmacy in West Beirut. Every now and then he would give me a ride on his bicycle on his way to or from the pharmacy. Later on, I met my wife in a building the Pilikians owned in Mar Mikhael neighborhood of Beirut. Her brother was my pharmacy school classmate. The family rented a flat on the first floor that had a balcony overlooking the busy street below.

It was through my request that Prof. Khachatur Pilikian forwarded me an electronic copy of his father's memoir through Dr. Dikran Abrahamian, the founder of Keghart.com website. The memoir is 249 pages long and is hand-written. He wrote it in a span of a quarter-of-a-century (July 25, 1960 to Nov. 25, 1985).

Israel Vahan Pilikian lived a long and productive life. He was born on June 21, 1902 and passed away in London at

95 on April 26, 1997. According to Prof. Pilikian, his father gave a testimonial at the Armenian Genocide commemoration in London just a day before his death.

Israel (Vahan) Pilikian was born to a hard-working, driven father who provided well for his family. He was 12 or 13 when he, along with his family, was driven for extermination. He had harrowing experiences. I would like to ask the readers to excuse me for noting the way he lost his sister, mother and father in that order when still in his teens so as to express the nature of his trauma and to justify the title of this article--that his odyssey was a triumphant overcoming over adversity.

Pilikian notes over and over again that they had become desensitized and had lost grip of the reality happening to them. The family gave their young daughter, Israel's youngest sister, away to give her a chance for survival when death, they thought, was imminent. The reality of the separation, however, soon set in and they frantically began to look for the person to whose trust they had placed their daughter so as to reclaim her. But their search was to no avail.

Israel's mother became "tongue-tied" after she and he were attacked and, at knifepoint, were forced to surrender the remaining gold coins they had wrapped around their bodies. She never spoke henceforth and remained in despair and would helplessly gaze at her children until her death that came not long after.

The horrible experiences rendered their once-vibrant father a recluse. On that fateful day Israel dreamt that his father, sleeping on the floor along with the rest of his remaining family members and other surviving relatives, was asking for water. He woke up and hurried to bring him a cup of water only to be confronted by the group's elders who told him that his father had died. It's under such circumstances that Israel Vahan Pilikian, his brother and sister embarked on their lives.

Israel Pilikian's life, much like that of many of his generation as survivors of the Genocide, was in the end, one of good overcoming evil, one of hope rather than hopelessness. These are not to be taken lightly. Thankfully, his children are highly appreciative of the legacy that has been handed down to them.

For a young boy whose schooling ended abruptly, Israel writes very well. He makes every effort to make his memoirs accurately depict his experiences. He does not shy away from mentioning that he does not remember a date, or the name of a place or how long a march lasted.

His memoirs resonated well with me especially when I read the passage where the family met its father anew after a forced separation in a town called Erayli in the province of Konya, a town my father-in-law would often mention because he was born there.

9. Righteous Turks from Erayli

Erayli is a name of a town in the province of Konya my late father-in-law would often mention. He was born there in 1915. Thanks to their Turkish friends and business partners, the family continued to live there until his father's untimely death sometime in the early 1920s.

Whenever he would reminisce about his childhood and tell us about Erayli, I would wander if such a humane townspeople existed in Turkey in 1915 let alone such a town. However I worded and sounded the name of the town I still could not find any reference to any town in Turkey that remotely sounded similar. For a while I thought of writing to a Turkish consulate to help me locate the town. I don't remember in what context it was that I appealed in a comment to readers of Keghart.com if they knew of such a town. Lo and behold I got a response. The name turned out to be Ereğli in the province of Konya, as my father-in-law would say. According to Wikipedia Ereğli (formerly Erekli) is a Turkish toponym derived from Ancient Greek Ἡράκλεια (Herakleia), in Latin Heraclea or Heraclia.

I do not read, write or speak Turkish. It may be that Ereğli is pronounced Erayli, but lingering doubt remained in me that my father-in-law may have forgotten the pronunciation of the town he was born in. My doubts dissipated when recently I read Israel Vahan Pilikian's memoir where he mentioned the name of a town in Armenian character that sounded exactly the way my father-in-law pronounced Erayli in the province of Konya in Turkey. Much like my late father-in-law, who would almost always refer the two jointly, Pilikian had done the same as well. I have not heard the sound of that name in Armenian from anyone else, nor read about the town in Armenian literature anywhere else.

Israel Vahan recounted that the Pilikian family found their father safe and sound in Erayli and reunited with him after the family was forcefully separated on their way to their 1915 golgotha.

It was a discovery that not only affirmed to me that my father-in-law correctly pronounced the name, it also affirmed to me all the good things he would say about his father's Turkish business partners in that town.

I do not use the word lightly because the discovery of those few lines in Mr. Pilikian's memoirs was eureka moment for me. It happened on a plane on our way to celebrate Thanksgiving with our son and his family. To kill time I was reading the Pilikian's memoir I had downloaded in my computer from the PDF file that I had received. I immediately pointed out the few lines to my wife. After reading those few lines, she said: "Lals yegav". It is commonly used expression in Armenian that means I am on the verge to cry.

My father-in-law passed away two decades ago and yet his experiences have left an indelible impression upon us. I think our instinctive emotional reaction to having heard of his birthplace from another Armenian survivor is common occurrence for the descendents of the survivors of the Genocide of the Armenians.

Ereğli İstasyon Caddesi 1920'lı Yıllarda

We know the following about my father-in-law. His father's name was Hovsep; his mother's name was Hripsime'. They had named their children Boghos, Mehran--my father-in-law-

-and their daughter Takouhie. I cannot help it, my eyes got teary as I wrote these names much like they did when I read my father-in-law's obituary in Clifton, New Jersey where he passed away and where he is buried far from Erayli. Such authentic Armenian names for what must have been a traditional Armenian family living on their ancestral lands for generations and carving a life for them by minding their own business, attending to their needs, striving to attain the niceties of life, if possible; and securing an honorable standing for themselves in the society they lived.

Upon the death his father and after continuing to live in the town for some time, his mother seeing that her children were growing up isolated from the rest of the Armenians and speaking only Turkish moved to Latakia, Syria in mid-'20s. Her sister was married to an Armenian pharmacist there whose family name was Margosian. Their business partners helped the young mother and her three children by escorting the family and seeing them board a ship to their destination.

Their family name was Altebarmakian. In Syria they were registered as Hovsepian after their father. The registering officer, apparently finding Altebarmakian difficult to write, decided to register them as Hovsepians after their deceased patriarch's name, Hovsep. Thus they severed all official ties with their past. In Latakia my father-in-law had a few years of schooling in the local Armenian school. Apparently the eminent Armenian writer Armen Anoush had taken a liking to the handsome kid with hazel eyes who only spoke Turkish. Mr. Anoush took upon himself to teach the boy Armenian with the correct pronunciation, my father-in-law would recall.

Years later, my father-in-law would continue telling us, that they received unexpected guests in the persons of his father's Turkish business partners and friends. It turned out that their Turkish family friends, having lost contact with them had embarked on a journey in search of the family. They had undertaken the search for a reunion of the families for old times sake. That is why I have carved a place of affection in my heart to a town named Erayli in the province of Konya in Turkey.

10. Wobbling Pillars

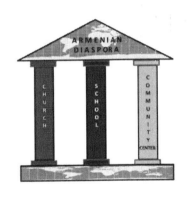

A recent editorial at Keghat.com noted that the Armenian school, one of the pillars that along with the church and the community center, constitutes the trinity that sustains the Armenian Diaspora, is wobbling. Seismic events not only wobbled pillars but have also toppled them.

During the last few decades the Armenian Diaspora has been experiencing the violent political upheavals in the Middle East, the cradle of the Armenian Diaspora. These events are endangering the very foundations of the communities and hence its schools. The economic recession in the Western World is also adversely affecting on the attendance to the Armenian Schools. More parents are sending their children to public schools instead because the Armenian schools are private and costlier. We have no control over these matters. The best we can do is to adjust.

Pillars wobble, if not topple, because the ground on which they were entrenched ceases to be the solid support it was once. The analogy refers to our evolving perception of Armenian schools. Two fundamental issues have always surfaced regarding an Armenian parents' rightful concerns about Armenian schools in North America or in the Middle East. The two concerns are the education their children would receive and the ease with which their children would be able to communicate with the larger society. The latter being not only the mastery of the larger society's language but also the ease of its conveyance, that is to say accent. A few years ago the late George Apelian, educator, author, pointed out to me that more affluent Armenian parents are sending their children to non-Armenian schools in Lebanon for this very reason.

Solid education and accent are valid concerns. Let's put them in perspective.

A few years ago I attended an annual conference that had to do with my specialization--pharmaceutics. People from all over the world attended the conference. To warm up his audience for a dry subject he was about to deliver, one of the lecturers asked: "What is the language of science?" He then answered it: "In the United States it's English spoken with an accent". How true. In this interdependent world, it's also Hindi, Mandarin or Arabic spoken with an accent as well. Those who have heard Vartan Gregorian or Arnold Schwarzenegger have surely noted that they speak with an accent. But that has not prevented them from reaching the uppermost echelon of society. In this increasingly flattened and interdependent world, no one really cares much about your accent as long as you offer what your interlocutor needs to forge a win-win relationship with you, be it personal or impersonal.

Capable teachers have transmitted solid education since antiquity in structurally much more modest environments and without the gadgetry modern schools enjoy. Computers are the outcome of such basic education and will never be able to replace it. Let us be mindful that those who brought about the computer revolution were schooled without the help of a monitor and its accompanying keyboard. Armenian schools historically have done well in imparting sold basic education to generations of students. I have yet to hear a naturalized friend or an acquaintance in the United States, Armenian descent or not, tell me in hindsight that he or she wished their parents had sent them to an all American school to better prepare them for life in their adopted country.

On the contrary, the overwhelming majority of former students in Armenian schools I have met fondly remember their times there. There is a reason for it and it has to do with EQ-- Emotional Quotient of these former students. EQ is a measurement of a person's ability to monitor his or her emotions, to cope with pressures and demands, and to control his or her thoughts and actions. Educators agree that EQ is as important as IQ (Intelligence Quotient).

There was a time when what students learned in a classroom stayed with them unchanged for a long time. Not anymore. Education is also learning to constantly learn new things. A student has to be emotionally well adjusted and prepared to surmount this ceaseless onslaught of newer things. Along with imparting solid and basic education, Armenian schools have been very successful in preparing their students to score higher in their EQ. Most of the students I knew in my formative years, while attending Armenian schools in Lebanon, have done well. In fact, they have done very well whether they attended college or not.

I do not want to paint a picture of an all-too-perfect Armenian school that does not exist. Institutions do not function in perfection. I simply want to elaborate on the issues of accent and of basic education so that parents would have a broader perspective should they be considering to enroll their children in an Armenian school.

Historically, Armenian schools have not failed us. On the contrary, they have successfully equipped their former students with basic knowledge and social anchor to venture out to make a living. After all, for us it has always been and will always be much like the often time quoated saying: *Our Hats Hon Gats*, which literally means: "wherever there is bread, that's where you stop".

11. Memorable Interview

My first job interview in America remains the more memorable among the many first time experiences I had in the New World after I landed at the J.F. Kennedy Airport on July 9, 1976. The weekend long Bicentennial Celebration had barely winded down. The interview was with the American Cyanamid Corporation, which has long folded away. According to Wikipedia it was a leading American conglomerate that became one of the nation's top 100 manufacturing companies during the 1970s.

Apprehensive as I was to be punctual and yet not too early, I lingered around the building and presented myself to the receptionist just few minutes before the appointment time. I was asked to wait, but the wait was getting longer than I thought it would. An ominous sign, I thought to myself. Who, I wandered, would take genuine interest and offer a job to a new comer like me who is not a local graduate and has no local work experience? Let alone to the fact that I had no experience in the field I wanted to make a career - pharmaceutics - other than relevant education.

I was immersed in my thoughts when a very distinguished looking gentleman stepped out and met me. He apologized for the delay and escorted me to his office and had me seated on a chair across his desk. He then welcomed me in Arabic to my total surprise. I asked him how is that he has learned Arabic. Adding further excitement to my initial surprise, he told me that he was born and raised in Lebanon and that his father was a longstanding employee of the American University of Beirut (AUB), my alma mater. We started chatting about Lebanon and AUB to break ice but I remained distracted at the sight of his nameplate on his desk facing me. It spelled his name, Robert Glockler. The last name appeared very familiar to me, even though it is not a common name one would ordinarily encounter. Looking back

I wander if my natural inclination to wander off had not become all too evident by my distraction to my detriment.

Some time back I translated my late uncle's – Dr. Antranig Chalabian's - narration in the late Antranig Dzarougian's weekly *Nairi* about the serendipitous events that lead to the publication of Dr. Stanley Kerr's book titled *The Lions of Marash*. The Kerrs resided in Trention, NJ. It turns out they socialized with the Glocklers. Henry Wilfrid Glockler was an employee of the American University of Beirut. Being a subject of Great Britain, an enemy nation, he was deported - for lack of a better word – 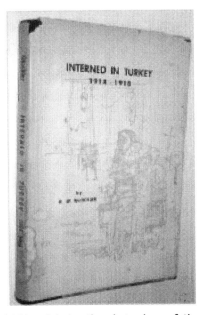 at the onset of the World War I into the interior of the Ottoman Empire. He thus became an eyewitness to the atrocities committed against the Armenian subjects of the Empire. He had his eyewitness accounts penned down. The manuscript that was written in 1918 had remained dormant in Henry W. Glockler's archives. Upon the recommendation of Dr. Stanley Kerr, he sent his manuscript to Antranig Chalabian who had the memoirs published as a book.

Having made a connection to the name on the nameplate I was facing I digressed the conversation and in the spur of the moment blurted out if he was by any chance related to Henry Glockler. From the looks of his face it became apparent that he was caught by surprise. He told me that Henry is his father and wondered how was it that I had heard of his name. Without going into the details, not mentioning that I had accompanied my uncle many a time to the printer's shop, nor did I mention that I had read the book, I said instead that Antranig Chalabian is my uncle. He responded something to the effect that it is a small world indeed and that he had heard so much about him from his father.

Henry Wilfrid Glockler, the father of my interviewer, authored *Interned in Turkey 1914-1918*. It was published in 1969 at Sevan Press in Beirut. It is 154 pages long memoir of the author. The book is "Dedicated To the thousands of innocent Armenian men, women and children of Ourfa, Turkey, who perished amid the horrors of the infamous [Armenian] genocide of 1915-18."

Both of these books, *The Lions of Marash* and *Interned in Turkey 1914-1918* were published at the aftermath of the 50th Anniversary commemoration of the Armenian Genocide. I remember vividly the community wide 50th Anniversary commemoration in the sport stadium named after the late Lebanese President Camille Chamoun. I believe that the occasion marked a turning point in the pursuit for the just resolution of the Armenian Genocide. It marked the end of our indoor mourning. The community seemed to have broken for good the shell that had confined it for so long. There was much excitement in the air that stemmed from a confidence that instinctively comes about after having overcome what may have appeared to be insurmountable odds.

As to my interview with Henry Wilfrid Glockler's son, Robert, it took a new turn. The formalities for the job interview gave way to a new discovered familiarity. He invited me for lunch at the company's cafeteria and I stayed with him in his office long after that.

Not too long after my interview, I got an invitation to the company's research facility in Princeton, NJ. When I presented myself there, I found out that all the department heads were lined up to interview me for a job opening commensurate with my education and the level of experience I had. I am sure that Robert Glockler had made that possible. I do not know how my interview went. Almost right after the interview I noted to the company that I received a job offer from the Schering-Plough Corporation that few years ago also ceased to exist as well. This time around it was thanks to another Armenian connection. Henry Apelian. He was a director at the company's international division. He recommended and presented me for an interview. I was offered a job that set me in my career path.

Dr. Antranig Chalabian, about whom I wrote in the first volume, passed away in 2011. I do not know if he ever became aware that the book he edited, found sponsors and had it published is now being retailed for hundreds of dollars on the Internet as an out of print rare book. I became a beneficiary of his interest in Armenian history.

My first job interview in America became a source of comfort for me. My immediate and extended family members were still in Lebanon. I was away from home and by myself, but I was not all alone.

12. There's No Respect - Յարգանք Չկայ

I hit the Control key...
so why am I not in control?

I was reminded of the title last week during my dealings with Vako, the programming wiz kid, as far as I am concerned, of Keghart.com. I had encountered some glitches. When I clicked on some of my earlier articles posted at Keghart.com, I got a notice that I am not authorized to access the page.

It was not only I who was not allowed access. Any other reader would not have been able to read the articles in question as well. I was trying to have Miss Effie Chambers inducted into Iowa Women's Hall of Fame. My first attempt was turned down last year. It was a close call I was told. But I was persisting and I need to have a wider audience read the two articles posted in Keghart.com. As far as I am concerned, Miss Chambers is an illustrious daughter of Iowa, well ahead of her time. She deserves her state's recognition.

Vako resolved the issue through persistent inquiries, all the while guiding me to let him know how, when and where I encountered the problem. There were many emails exchanged. There may not have been the need to send so many emails had I been able to communicate with Vako in technical terms. I told him in one of our early emails that when it comes to technical terms related to the cyber world, I am a dinosaur like creature. That's when I was reminded over again of what some of my generation tell me that there is no respect for the ageing seniors any more.

There was a time when the patriarch of a family would have inherited land from his father. In time he would have passed it to his children, especially to his sons. Over the years, the father would have also accumulated knowledge his sons would need as how to best till the land. A whole lot has changed these days, thanks to the technological advances driven by the young and the restless in the persons of Jobs, Wozniak, Gates and others.

These young nerds were crazy enough to think they can change the world, and they did, as Jobs said. They helped pave the way to mega farms, superstores such as Wal-Mart, wiping away the small farms, mom-and-pop businesses that at one time constituted the core of the average family's livelihood that would have passed on to the next generation. The late Sam Walton, sitting in his office in front of a computer, with a click to a button on his key board, would have had all sorts of figures displayed in front of his eyes coming from any of the many and many stores he owned anywhere in world. Such centralized and readily accessible knowledge was not possible few decades ago.

The Baby Boomers, born on January 1, 1946 onward, hit the magical number 65 on January 1, 2011. There again 65 is a number that is outdated and has no relevance any more. It was the acceptable retirement age at one time into one's so called "golden years". That is not true any more. Officially retirement kicks in at the age of 66 in the U.S. for the Baby Boomers. You may collect pension as early as at the age of 62 for early retirement or as late as at 70. Naturally, your pension changes accordingly. However, these two extreme numbers revolve around the magical number of 66. There again, it is not a static world any more, but the upcoming fluid world. The younger you are the older your retirement age will be. It increases in increments of months.

For all the Baby Boomers out there, much like me, I have some advice. Brace as you step into a world far away from the cushion and the cocoon that was your work and world. Do not expect respect. It's true that banks and restaurants offer perks to seniors, but those perks are not bestowed upon the seniors out of respect. The banks, the restaurants and the like want their business, that's all. They will do anything to entice you to dispense off your golden eggs, if you were able to build a golden egg nest, that is. Learn to respect your children, and your grandchildren. You will need them to program the blinking time on your microwave oven or VCR or program your other household utensils, let alone the devices in your car. Where on earth did the words "Apple," 'Bluetooth," "BlackBerry" come about to mean what they mean these days?

Your children and grandchildren have a lot to teach you in this topsy-turvy and crazy world. Respect them and be content with your lot. Respect is due to those who have the skill and the knowledge many of my generations do not posses. Respect is not lost. It is still around but it has shifted and reversed the generational gear.

13. The Case for Community Nursing Home

It is said that a scientist wanted to study the effect of electric shock on roaches. So he administered a jolt of electricity to the roach and measured how high it jumped. He then severed one of its legs and did the same and continued on doing so until all the legs were severed while measuring all the while how high the roach jumped when given the electric shock. He then concluded that the roach loses its sensitivity to electric shock as its legs are severed. Data can lead to such interpretation.

I was reminded of this story after having read Viken L. Attarian's guest-editorial in Keghart.com about the need and use of demographic database. He states: "for example, there have been several attempts in the past and even recently to create Armenian retirement homes or homes for the elderly, the argument being that our elderly do not speak English or French and prefer to be with other Armenians (services to include Armenian cooking, church services and Armenian traditional activities). While this might have been the case 30-40 years ago, there is no scientific evidence that suggests that this is true today, i.e. that 10 years from now we would actually have a group of retirees who would want, need and be ready to finance such an effort. We could be wasting a lot of resources raising the funds to build such an institution but it could be simply another enormous waste of our resources."

On a positive note I thought this might lead to healthy discussion regarding the need for more assisted living and skilled nursing within the Armenian community.

To give some structure to my train of thoughts I would like to have the following introduction. I served on the board of trustees of the Home for the Armenian Aged, Inc. in Emerson, NJ for a decade. My last board meeting was the evening prior to my departure day, as the company I would work for relocated me first and months later my family. That makes my last board meeting in March 1995 and which brings my first board meeting more than 25 years ago. Those ten years as a member of the Board of Trustees became an education for me. My father's last year was in a nursing home in Los Angeles, not at the Ararat Nursing Facility where presently my mother resides. Eventual need for a nursing home looms large for any one of us.

I would also like to note that there was a time in my youth when I considered Diaspora transient on our way to settle in Armenia. I admit I had utopian and euphoric notions of a homeland. Diaspora will be my lasting place. A nursing home in Armenia for Diaspora Armenians is not a viable option. Who among us would want to leave family and friends behind and move to Armenia to spend the twilight of his or her later years there?

It would be a wrong notion to visualize an Armenian nursing or assisted living home are or can be run by an Armenian staff all through. It is very likely, while some of the professionals such as doctors; nurses, administrators etc. may be Armenian but not necessarily Armenian speaking. The majority of the staff, be it nurses' aides, dietary workers, activities assistants, housekeeping more likely than not will not be speaking or understanding Armenian. Even then you need to be conversant in English to communicate with all those involved in daily care. Not being proficient in English or French for Canadian Armenians are not relevant to the need of having retirement homes within the community at large.

Community financing of an Armenian nursing home, as an added financial burden to the community, may also be mischaracterization without defining as to what the financing entails. Obviously nursing homes function under strict federal, state or government guideline. There is state assistance by way of Medicare or Medicaid in case of U.S.A. It is not uncommon that even for the financially well off, their savings may eventually get depleted as they may outlive their savings and will need to rely on government assistance. Obviously community sponsored nursing homes entail erecting the facility and managing it. I do not mean to say administering it. The latter is for certified nursing home administrators. In The United States there are Armenian community supported nursing homes in Massachusetts, New York, New Jersey, Michigan and California. However, I do not think they are sufficient to meet the needs for caring the aged.

Why the case for community nursing homes then, when all function under the same guidelines? In my view community nursing homes render better quality care. They are by the very nature of their founding under the watchful eyes and scrutiny of the community. They become magnets where school children go to entertain the residents, dignitaries to visit, priests to render mass and have the religious holidays observed. Many auxiliary groups congregate around the ethnic nursing homes and there is a better pool of volunteers. Well beyond the language issues there are real life advantages for having community nursing homes, they provide better care.

The Home for the Armenian Aged, Inc. in Emerson, NJ was founded in 1938 and became operational five years later. At its 50th anniversary in 1993, I researched and wrote the story of its founding and progress the community made from its formative years, maintaining a chicken coop and growing their own vegetables for the residents' use, to the veritable institution it had become fifty years later

My concluding remarks stay viable nowadays as it did then. I quote: "The sociologist claim that we are heading towards a graying society and statistical projections predict that an increasing number of the population will need the care of a nursing home in the twilight of their later years. Also there was a large influx of Armenians in the mid-seventies from Middle East and what was the former Soviet Union, who in case of need, most likely will seek the familiarity of their ethnic nursing homes. Such trends indicate that the Home will continue to function as a viable institution well into the twenty first century. However, members of the community need to continue to assume responsibility of managing the Home prudently and soundly. The ever escalating cost of health care, and the dwindling financial resources, paradoxically coupled with increasing compliance standards, ever so more will require the continual community management and support to keep the spirit and the purpose of its Founders alive and viable, to meet the needs of the once productive citizens of this nation"

14. A Rebel With A Cause

Those who know the mild-mannered musicologist Bedros Alahaidoyan would never dream of using the adjective "rebel" to describe him. Please give the benefit of a doubt and read on.

I met him for the first time in 2010. He and his wife had graciously accepted our invitation for a lunch at my mother's house in Los Angeles. However, I knew of Bedros long before that.

In the '50s and the '60s there was a pharmacy in Beirut called *Pharmacie de la Paix*. It was also known among the

Armenian community as *խաղաղութեան Դեղարան* *(Khaghaghoutian Tegharan, i.e. Pharmacy of Peace),* It was one of the most prominent pharmacies in the commercial hub of the city center. It was on Rue Weygand, not far from the Lebanese Parliament, in an area known for its cluster of the big banks. Much like the rest of the Armenian businesses, the pharmacist owner was referred to by his phamacy's name more so by his. It is thus that I came to know of Bedros Alahaidoyan as *Pharmacie de la Paix*'s son who was not interested in his father's thriving business but instead pursued "music" in Europe.

Bedros's interest did not seem to make much sense or sit well with the members of the downtown's Armenian business community who knew and related to each other much like the members of a clan would, even though they competed ferociously in business. They were a business force to reckon with, if not the predominant businessmen of the area. Their opinion mattered. My father worked at and later ran Hotel Lux on Allenby Street, a walking distance from the Pharmacy where I had been many times with him. He would never fail to point out to me how good the lot of a pharmacist could be in Beirut.

The '60s was the era of the Woodstock, "do not trust anyone over thirty" and the "flower power" generation. Music to the young and the restless of the '60s was an instrument of the counterculture, if you will. It was the era of rebels without much of a cause. Not having met him in person, I thought of Bedros, as the son of the well-to-do family, pursuing his "thing" in Europe. Little did I know of what I found over the last decade or two about Bedros' real vocation during those years. I realize now how wrong my perceptions of him were then.

It turns out tht Bedros did study pharmacy in Belgium but rather than engage in the profession he continued his studies in music. He graduated as a musicologist from the State University in Brussels and worked at the state-run radio to support his mission salvaging Armenian folk songs from their inevitable loss due to the passing away of the displaced survivors of the Genocide.

Since early '70s Bedros embarked on his mission collecting Armenian folk songs. Initially he collected the folk songs of Kurdified Armenians who had settled in Belgium and in Holland. He then expanded his search by visiting other European, American and Middle Eastern cities and their Armenian seniors' homes. His decades-long endeavors culminated in 2009 in the publication *Բալուի եւ Տարածաշրջանի Երաժշտական Ազգագրական Հաւաքածոյ (An Ethno-Musicological Collection of Palou and its Neighboring Areas)*.

The book is in hard cover with a dust jacket depicting an actual Armenian inscription in Palou (Palu), a historic Armenian enclave. The book is written in Western Armenian and is printed in Yerevan, Armenia with easily readable fonts over good quality white paper. One does not need to be a musicologist to be impressed by the depth and breath of the book. With this book Bedros Alahaidoyan salvaged for posterity a vast collection of the folk songs of Palou that were passed down to singer Maro Nalbandian.

The 448-pages long book consists of three parts.

The first part is a collection of six articles dealing with the history of Palou and its traditions. Black and white and color pictures depict Palou then and now. This section also contains a fairly large compilation of folk songs that Bedros Alahaidoyan has collected through the years. The texts of folk songs from more than 30 historical Armenian villages are listed.

The second part is a textual and musicological presentation of the seventy-two Palou folk songs in the collection. The notes and the lyrics of each of these songs are laid out. An explanatory note accompanies each.

The third part contains various lists and catalogues such as dictionary of rural dialects, bibliography, locations from which the songs have been collected and the list of the songs in the two compact discs that accompany the book.

The two CDs are voiced by Maro Nalbandian and are attached to the inner cover of the book. There is no instrument accompanying the songs to preserve the authenticity of the folk songs.

The book along with the two CDs retail for $75.00 and can be purchased from Abril or Sardarabad bookstores in Glendale, CA or may requested from the author.

Treading along the pioneering path of Gomidas Vartabed, who is considered to be one of the pioneers of ethnomusicology, has led Bedros to another discovery in the person of his wife Violet, the daughter of Nartouhie Khosrofian from the Sgham village of Palou. Bedros has dedicated his book to her and attributes its realization to her encouragement and support.

Alahaidoyans live in Glendale, California where Bedros pursues his calling with the same youthful passion and the continued support of his wife Violet.

15. Love During the *Medz Yeghern*

The award-winning novelist Chris Bohjelian published his *Sandcastle Girls* novel in 2012. The upcoming publication of the novel was heralded in the Armenian media. Readers waited the printing with much anticipation. The Armenian American community enthusiastically received the book and its author. ANCA awarded Chris Freedom Award for his work educating English language readers about the Armenian Genocide. His Holiness Aram I, Catholicos of the Great House of Cilicia bestowed upon him Saint Mesrob Mashdots Medal.

A quarter of century before the publication of the *Sandcastle Girls*, the eminent novelist Antranig Dzarougian published in 1987 a novel titled *Սէրը Եղեռնին Մէջ (Sereh Yeghernin Metch, i.e. Love in the Yeghern)*. The book is in Western Armenian. Its publication did not capture the Armenian media's attention or stir the public's imagination the way *Sandcastle Girls* did, although the book is superbly readable. Media outlets in 1987 were altogether different and did not have the modern capabilities for mass promotion.

Both of these novels are love stories during the Armenian Genocide, although with the *Sandcastle Girls* no such inference can be made reading the title unlike with Dzarougian's book. "Մեծ Եղեռն" (Medz Yeghern) is a term that the survivors coined for the Armenian Genocide. The verbatim translation of the term would be "The Great Crime" but the word "Yeghern" has also an inherent sadness embedded in it that the English word "crime" would not convey. No other Armenian synonym has ever come close to connote and embody the horrors of the Genocide the way the term "Medz Yeghern" does. No wonder that the eminent novelist Antranig Dzarougian opted to use the term for titling his book instead of the Armenan word for Genocide.

Sandcastle Girls is a story within a story of fictional characters. Amazon.com describes it this way: "When Elizabeth Endicott arrives in Aleppo, Syria, she has a diploma from Mount Holyoke, a crash course in nursing, and only the most basic grasp of the Armenian language. It's 1915, and Elizabeth has volunteered to help deliver food and medical aid to refugees of the Armenian Genocide during the First World War. There she meets Armen, a young Armenian engineer who has already lost his wife and infant daughter. After leaving Aleppo and traveling into Egypt to join the British Army, he begins to write Elizabeth letters, realizing that he has fallen in love with the wealthy young American. Years later, their American granddaughter, Laura, embarks on a journey back through her family's history, uncovering a story of love, loss—and a wrenching secret that has been buried for generations."

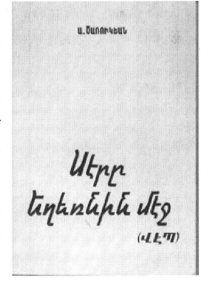

Love in the Yeghern is based on the true love story of the eminent early 20th century Armenian poet Roupen Sevag and his wife Yanno. He was a medical doctor and an accomplished painter as well.

The novel is a true depiction of their lives and a fictional rendering of their interactions and stands vis-à-vis the cultural and political affairs of the Armenians in the Ottoman Empire. Most of the other characters in the book are also depictions of prominent Istanbul Armenians of the era. The characters are referred to either by their first or family names. Anyone who has a basic knowledge of Western Armenian culture that blossomed after remaining dormant for centuries and hit its zenith just before the Genocide, would not have difficulty surmising who Dzarougian refers to when he makes reference to characters in his novel named Varoujan, Adom, Zartarian and many others.

Roupen (Chilingirian) Sevag was born in Silvri, Ottoman Turkey on February 15, 1885. After graduating from the famed Berberian Armenian School in Istanbul he moved to Lousanne, Switzerland where he studied medicine and fell in love with a vibrant woman named Yanni. After Roupen's graduation the couple returned to Istanbul in 1914. Roupen's German born and raised wife Yanni supported her husband's decision to return home to be with his people. Their decision would end up costing Roupen his life. He was arrested a year later at the onset of the Armenian Genocide on April 24, 1915 and was tortured to death on August 26,

1915 along with Taniel Varoujan, Siamanto and others. He was 30 years old.

Roupen Sevag is known for his patriotic and humanistic poetry. According to Wikipedia he also composed many love songs, which were highly acclaimed for their feeling and depth, He is fondly remembered to this day. In 2011 a stamp was issued in Armenia featuring him. There is a school in Yerevan named after him. A family museum, established and run by his nephew, was relocated in 2012 from Nice, France to the Holy Etchmiazin in Armenia.

Janine, the fictional heroine of the book and the widow of the novel's central tragic figure Roupen, much like his wife Yanni, felt betrayed by her own people for their complicity with the Turks in annihilating her husband and his people. She returned to Europe and vowed not raise her children with a Germanic culture. She settled in France and published in French. The French Academy cited her for one of her works much like it did to Yanni in the real world.

Dzarougian ends his novel depicting Janine and writes: "She lived engrossed in her books and in her children Levon and Shamiram. With the passing years ashes covered her hair, but not her heart. Her heart remained fresh and vibrant defying time and years with an indifference but always open, always graceful on white pages and in her thoughts with her Roupen.....".

Kourken Mekhitarian has noted in his review of Armenian literature that after his death, Roupen emerged as a tragic but an iconic and a heroic larger than life figure and that his life could be the subject of a captivating novel. Antranig Dzarougian's novel *Love in the Yeghern* makes for a captivating reading and renders justice to this young couple's love and life stories.

The novel awaits translation on the eve of the centennial of the Armenian Genocide, the Medz Yeghern.

16. Remembering Simon Simonian

Simon Simonian was one of the towering intellects and literary figures of the Armenian Diaspora's post-Genocide century. He was an educator, publisher, editor, author, and an activist.

He was born on March 24, 1914 in Aintab. His Sassoun-born father's name was Ove'. His mother's name was Menoush. She hailed from Aintab. Sassoun was once an exclusively Armenian-inhabited highland while Aintab (now Gaziantep) had a large Armenian population. Simonian was their eldest child.

In 1921, having survived the Genocide, the family found refuge in Aleppo. The future writer-publisher received his elementary education in that city in northern Syria. Subsequently, he attended (1930-1935) the newly established seminary of the Catholicosate of Cilicia in Antelias, Lebanon becoming one of its first students.

After graduating from the seminary he returned to Aleppo where he taught at the Gulbenkian and Haigazian Schools until 1946. During the war years he established with a group of like-minded Armenian teachers a printing press he named "Sevan".

At the invitation of Catholicos Karekin I Hovsepiants (1946) he moved to Lebanon where he taught at the catholicosate's seminary until 1955 and became the institute's scholar in residence. He also established a close personal and professional relationship with the Catholicos. His scholarly contributions during those years and later are far too numerous to list.

In 1954 he visited Armenia as a member of the delegation representing the Catholicosate of Cilicia at the funeral of Catholicos Kevork VI Tcheorekdjian. At the time a visit to the Soviet Republic was considered an extraordinary event. That visit became a life altering experience for him. The following year he resigned from his positions at the catholicosate but continued teaching, part-time, for many years at the Armenian General Benevolent Union affiliated Hovagimian-Manougian Secondary School for Boys and at the Tarouhie Hagopian Secondary School for Girls.

In 1955 he reestablished his Sevan printing press so as to have his own voice heard. Three years later he launched a literary magazine he named "Spurk", which means Diaspora. It along with Antranig Dzarougian's literary weekly named "Nayiri" became prominent literary magazines and platforms for many authors and budding writers.

Along with his teaching and scholarly research Simonian wrote Armenian history, geography and language textbooks for different grades. They were reprinted several times and became standard textbooks at Armenian schools across the Diaspora.

Simonian authored the following novels and collection of short stories: կը խնդրուի խաչամերել *(Obstruction Requested, 1965)*; խմբապետ Ասլանի Աղջիկը *(Commander Aslan's Daughter, 1967)*; Լեռնականներու Վերջալոյսը *(The Sunset of the Mountaineers, 1968)*; Սիփանայ Քաջեր *(The Daredevils of Sipan, 1967-1970)*; Լեռ եւ ճակատագիր *(Mountain and Fate, 1972)*; Անժամանորոս *(UntimelyMan, 1978, 1998)*.

Simonian was not hamstrung by Armenian political partisanship. He possessed a too large personality and a streak of Sassountsi free spirit to be confined by partisanship. His concern for all things Armenian resonated across the Diaspora political spectrum and he became a much-loved personality. I recall with fond memories the overwhelming popular reception he received in the social hall of New Jersey's St. Vartanants Cathedral when he and his wife were invited to tour the Armenian communities in the United States in the early '80s.

After reading his books it becomes apparent that his father's lineage from the Armenian highland of Sassoun shaped his literary imagination and his perception of what an Armenian is or ought to be. Many of the stories of his books depict the once-proud mountaineers of Sassoun as heroes. Driven from their mighty highlands, the generous spirit of these proud mountaineers would find outlets as bakers in the bakeries they ran in Aleppo, setting up a tradition that continues to this day.

Simonian had a commanding presence even though he was not tall. Anyone who has had the opportunity to call him couldn't forget his deep baritone that came over the wires with his customary greeting "Ողջույն" (voghjuyn). The closest word for it in English is salute but surely his *voghjuyn* embodied more than a mere salutation.

Several times I had the pleasure of calling him at his office. When I recall those moments I realize that he must have assumed that his world was inhabited only by Armenians and hence his greeting *voghjuyn* instead of hello. The latter makes deference to the caller's native language and offers the courtesy of the doubt and greets the caller in a universally accepted manner. But it was always *voghjuyn* for Simonian.

He was married to Aleppo-born Mary Ajemian. Much like his heroes, she also hailed from a Sassountsi family. She was the sister of Kevork Ajemian, a well-known bilingual (Armenian and English) journalist and novelist. The Simonians had four sons (Hovig, Vartan, Daron and Sassoun) and a daughter Maral.

Simonian died on March 24, 1986. Armen Tarian's eulogy in *Zartonk* daily (March 29, 1986) borrowed Simonian's greeting and wrote: *"Voghjuyn* Simon. "Sevan" Press was his Lake of Sevan. Not only its ambience , but simply its name would transform him". (Ողջոյն Սիմոն: Տպարան «Սեւան»ը իր Սեւանայ լիճն էր, ոչ միայն անոր մթնոլորտը, այլ անոր անունն անգամ կը հոգեփոխէր զինք).

The boy who learned business on the streets of Aleppo proved to be an astute entrepreneur as well, successfully running his business for at least two decades publishing in addition to his books, textbooks, "Spurk" Weekly and other journals and periodicals more than 500 book titles including *Interned in Turkey 1914-1918*.

Sevan Press and its owner-publisher became landmark institutions in the Diaspora. Dignitaries visiting Lebanon made a point of meeting him. Unfortunately, almost ten years before his death, his much-beloved printing house became another casualty of the Lebanese Civil War and ceased being the outlet for his prodigious literary output.

Simon Simonian's literary legacy remains an enduring part of the post-Genocide Western Armenian literature.

17. Shahnoor: Doomster of Western Armenians

The year 2014 marked the 40th anniversary of the death of Shahan Shahnoor, one of the most celebrated writers of post-Genocide Western Armenian literature. The Istanbul-born writer remains immortalized particularly for his nove *Նահանջը Առանց Երգի (Retreat Without Song)* than the sum total of his literary opus.

The book is hailed as an epic and as such is much cited even today. At the dawn of the centennial of the Genocide it is considered more prophetic than ever. Some now consider the alarm the book sounded eighty-four years ago a fait accompli. The Western Armenian culture is in a precipitous and perilous decline.

In his famous book Shahnoor wrote: 'We are retreating, parent, child, uncle and groom; customs, understanding, morals and love are retreating. The language is retreating; the language is retreating; the language is retreating. We all are retreating with work and deed, willingly and unwillingly, knowingly and unknowingly; mea culpa to Mount Ararad...... The children, who could have grown up as future generations and would have come after us, are the last ransoms. Because those who will come will be strangers in work and in deed, willingly and unwillingly, knowingly and unknowingly; mea culpa to Mount Ararad......"

The novel is about the lot of Bedros, an Armenian boy having survived the Genocide, has found refuge in Paris, Gallicized his name to Pierre and is working as an apprentice at a photographer's studio. Pierre is also sexually involved with the owner of the studio, a voluptuous woman who goes by the name Mme. (Mrs.) Jeanne, although she is single. The descriptions of his sexual exploits were and may still be regarded daring by the standards of Armenian literature. It may also be the only modern Western Armenian novel to have been considered for censorship.

Pierre socializes with a group of expatriate Armenians like him who muse about the fate of their people as they become more and more assimilated and get less involved in the Armenian community. The intertwined and convoluted life of Pierre is what has made the book an Armenian masterpiece

Shahnoor was born in 1903. His baptismal name was

Shahnoor Kerestejian. After receiving his elementary education at the neighborhood school, he graduated from the famed Berberian School in 1921.

He was mostly self-educated. His maternal uncle, Teotig, who was celebrated for his yearly almanac, is claimed to have influenced the budding writer and poet. Almost right after graduation Shahnoor began to dabble in literature by posting translations in Armenian newspapers.

By 1923 it had become evident that the pan-nationalist movement would propel Mustafa Kemal, the future Ataturk, to the helm of the emerging Republic of Turkey and continue the persecution of minorities. Shahnoor left for Paris that year joining the exodus of other Western Armenian writers. To earn a living he worked at a photographer's studio but continued to write.

In 1929 he published *Նահանջը Առանց Երգի, կամ Պատկերազարդ Պատմութիւնը Հայոց* (*Retreat Without Song or the Illustrated History of the Armenians*). The book had been launched in installments in *Յառաջ* (*Haratch, i.e. Forward*) the leading Armenian newspaper in Paris.

Since its publication Shahnoor's masterpiece has been much referenced and its author frequently quoted. His contemporary writes did not necessarily embarce Shahnoor's gloomy prophecy. The book was published at a time when expatriated Armenian writers in France brought a new luster to post-Genocide Western Armenian literature.

The famed editor Shavarsh Missakian founded *Haratch* in 1925. The newspaper soon became known for attracting high-profile Armenian literary figures. His daughter Arpik took over the paper after his death in 1957. The paper folded in 2009 because of dwindling readership.

Poor in health, Shahnoor published his next novel in 1937. His malady, thought to have been osteoporosis, progressed rapidly causing him great pain. By 1939 he had lost his house and had become homeless and was confined to a sanitarium.

ԱՐՄԷՆ ԼԻՒՊԷՆ
ՇՈՒՐՋՐ ՈՉԻՆՉ

After recovering some of his health, Shahnoor began writing in French under the pen name Armen Lubin. "From then on he was acclaimed highly as a French writer and poet and received several literary awards," notes Wikipedia. He was distraught by what he considered a lack of support--if not outright neglect--of Armenian writers. However, Shahnoor did not severe his links with his roots and culture. He wrote several more books in Armenian. He died in 1974. The centennial of his birthday was commemorated in Armenia.

While there is renewed interest in *Retreat Without Song* novel, the book has never faded from the Armenian literary radar. The Western Armenian language is indeed retreating. Recently UNESCO classified it among endangered languages.

Many factors are contributing to the demise of the language. The deadly political events in the Middle East during the past five decades and the social unrest in these restive host countries have seriously undermined the

Armenian communities in Egypt, Lebanon, Iran, Jerusalem, and now also in Syria and Iraq. These organized and entrenched communities had in their heyday vast educational and social networks and were regarded (some still are) as the best guarantors of our millennia-old Western Armenian culture.

Renewed echoes of Shahnoor's predictions continue to be heard. Alluding to the younger generation born in the West, Rev. Hovhannes Sarmazian wrote recently: "Right in front of our very own eyes, with music and dance, we are losing them."

There can be no doubt that the Western Armenian language is endangered. A vivid example of the calamity is this article. To inform Armenians born or living in the West, who mostly do not read Armenian, it is written in English.

Whether Shahnoor and Rev. Sarmazian are prophetic in their lament for the inevitable loss of the culture and hence of the Armenian identity (because of the loss of our native language), will continue to be debated as succeeding generations measure events and developments with their own yardsticks.

18. An Undisputable Expert

There may still be some mulberry trees left in Keurkune and in greater Kessab. In my days most of the mulberry trees seemed to function as support to the grape vines. Both seemed to almost always been planted next to each other. The mulberry trees otherwise did not have much of other use. Their leaves were used as animal feed in an attempt to make use of them because the trees where there. Their berries were used for occasional savoring and for nothing else. The skin pulled from their branches made excellent ropes. These uses did not justify devoting space to grow them. They were planted at one time for an altogether different reason. Mulberry trees made possible the most import source for monetary income in greater Kessab. Their leaves were used to grow silkworms.

My fascination with silkworm cocoons has its roots to my early childhood days in our grandparent's house in Keurkune. Its ceiling was covered with logs that were blackened over time. Among these logs there were few silkworm cocoons that were lodged and had remained there out of reach for years, if not decades. These cocoons, tarnished over time, stirred my imagination as I lay on the bed. My grandparents had raised silkworm at one time to support raising their two sons, my father and my paternal uncle.

In her yet to be published auitobiography, Mrs. Effie Chambers, the beloved missionary of Kessab, lamented the loss of silk worms when reminiscing about her mission at the aftermath of the 1909 pogrom and sacking of Kessab. She wrote, "It was a most desolate picture that greeted my eyes. Houses had been burned after being looted, and silk worm eggs in the hatching process (one of the principal financial resources of the region) had been destroyed."

The silk worms are sedentary and are completely dependent on being fed mulberry tree leaves. They are voracious and selective eaters as well, eating non-stop only the leaves of white mulberry trees. No wonder the berries of the mulberry trees in Keurkuen were always white

I quote Wikipedia: "After the silkworm eggs hatch and yield 1/8 inch-long larva that start eating mulberry tree leaves. They must be fed constantly. Over the next 2 months, they will reach a full size of 2 inches, having molted (shed their "skin" and growing) four times in the process. They then spend 5 days spinning a cocoon. The cocoon is composed of silk that is made in 2 silk glands within the body. The single threads from each gland are formed into a double thread by the silkworm's mouthparts and spun around the body, totally encasing it. The continuous thread is hundreds of feet in length. Within 5 days of completing the cocoon the larva changes into a pupa and after another 20 – 24 days emerges as a moth. The moth escapes from the cocoon by emitting a liquid that digests away the silk enabling the moth to crawl out. The adult moths have no mouthparts and while they can flutter their wings, they cannot fly. After mating the male dies. Soon after laying her 300 eggs, the female also dies." I presume the eggs are collected and kept for next year's growth.

Over centuries silkworms were thus domesticated to the point that their survival was completely depended on human intervention. The knowledge for raising silk worms on a large scale became a valued learned art. Kessabtsis mastered the intricacies and the know-how and passed it from one generation to the next. After their return, the survivors of the Genocide seem to have managed to procure anew the essentials and continued raising silkworms. When they repatriated to Soviet Armenia in 1947, they carried their learned art with them and appeared to have helped the Soviet Union improve its silk production.

Mrs. Azniv (Talimian) Khederian was the late mother of Haigaz Khederian who is a cousin and the closest relative to my late paternal grandmother Sarah, nee Mousajekian. Haigaz repatriated to Soviet Armenia in 1947 with his parental family. His mother Azniv became the recipient of the highest orders Soviet Union bestowed upon its most distinguished denizens in arts and sciences. She was pinned with two medals, one bearing the likeness of the Soviet Star and the other bearing the likeness of Lenin's profile, the founder of the Soviet Order.

She received these orders for contributing to the cultivation of silkworms in Soviet Armenia that appeared to have greatly helped increase the production of silk in the Soviet Union. An art she had mastered in Kessab.

19. Siamanto's Dance

Սիամանթո
1878-1915

There is a poetic description of a dance in the Armenian literature that will remain forever etched in the Armenian psyche. One of its lines is often quoted in English or in Armenian, "O human justice, let me spit on your forehead". The line sounds more poignant in Armenian than in English and perhaps in other languages as well. It is by the eminent Armenian poet Siamanto who described the dance of twenty young Armenian women in his unforgettable "The Dance". The translation of the poem by Peter Balakian and Nevart Yaghlian is attached.

The poem is often recited at commemorations of the Armenian Genocide, although it was written five years before 1915, the beginning of the Genocide. Its most graphic image probably is the scene in film director's Atom Egoyan's "Ararat". There again, it was presented to depict the horrors of the Genocide. Meanwhile, Armenian painters have depicted "The Dance" in canvas. Most lasting, of course, is its life-long etching in the memory of Armenian high school students who are taught the poem and about its celebrated author.

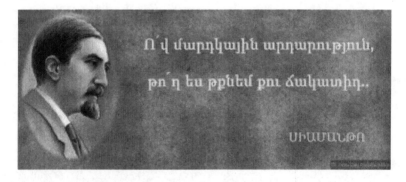

Siamanto published the poem in his book titled *Կարմիր Լուրեր Բարեկամէս* (*Garmir Lourer Pareghames, i.e. Bloody News From My Friend*). I used to wander why Siamanto gave the book such an odd title. Whenever I inquired about it, the customary explanation given to me amounted to no more than repetiting the title. It would take me decades to uncover the answer. It happened mid-way reading *The Black Dog of Fate*, the book that propelled Peter Balakian to the pinnacle of the Armenian-American literature, if not American literature as well. The book is as much an American experience as it is Armenian.

Peter Balakian elaborates on the turn of events that lead to the naming of the Siamanto's book in his and Nevart Yaghlian's translation of Siamento's book. In the introduction Balakian wrote that while growing up, he had heard, during family conversations, that his grandfather, who had died more than a decade before he was born, had something to do with a book of poetry very famous among the Armenians.

Peter Balakian's grandfather Diran and Adom Yarjanian, the baptismal name of Siamanto, were friends 'and came from middle- to upper-middle class families. Both went to Europe to further their studies. Diran studied medicine in Leipzig (Germany) and Yarjanian literature in Paris.

Diran returned to Constantinople in 1905 and started practicing medicine. In 1909, he went with a group of Armenian physicians, to Adana to help the survivors of one of the worst large-scale atrocities and killing perpetrated against the Armenians of the Ottoman Empire. The tragedy is known in Armenian history as the Adana Massacre. The calamity was not confined to that city although it started there. It is estimated that the Turkish marauding crowds slaughtered some 30,000 Armenians. The massacre is lamented in a song that is sung to this day. It is called *Ողբ Ադանայի* (*Voghp Adanayi, i.e The Lament of Adana)* and may be heard on Youtube.

Diran Balakian recorded in letters his eyewitness accounts. Unfortunately, the letters were lost. There seem to be two accounts as to how his friend Yarjanian came to know of the massacre first hand. In one version, Diran wrote to the poet. In another version, Balakian wrote home to his parents and Adom, being a family friend, read the letters when he visited them. In any event, it is to the news from Peter Balakian's paternal grandfather that Siamanto referred to in the title of his book.

Adom Yarjanian, better known by his pen name Siamanto, was born on August 15, 1878 in Agn, on the Euphrates River. He lived there with his parents until the age 14. It is during these formative years that he showed talent in writing poetry and was endearingly nicknamed Siamanto. He ended up using the moniker for the rest of his life. Strangely enough, nowadays aspiring young Armenian poets are also sometimes affectionately called Siamanto.

The family moved to Constantinople (Istanbul) in 1891 where Adom continued his studies at the famed Berberian School. He graduated in 1896, during the massacres in the interior of the country. The slaughter, now referred to as the Hamidian Massacres, claimed the lives of 250,000 to 300,000 Armenians. Like many other Armenian intellectuals, Yarjanian also fled the country in fear of persecution.

Siamanto also seemed to have been driven by wanderlust. After finishing his studies at the Sorbonne University in Paris, he moved to Cairo, Zurich, and Geneva where he contributed to the Тросиик (*Troshag, i.e. Flag*) journal, the organ of the Armenian Revolutionary Federation party. He then returned to Constantinople where he became privy to eyewitness accounts of the atrocities against the Armenians in the southeast of the country. From 1909 to 1911 he lived in Watertown, Massachusetts as editor of the Հայրենիք (*Hairenik, i.e. Fatherland*) daily. He published *Bloody News From My Friend* in 1910. He then traveled to the Caucasus before returning to Constantinople where he was arrested on the eve of April 24, 1915, along with other prominent Armenian literary and community leaders.

Siamanto did not appear to have been distracted by his wanderlust. It might even have helped to boost his creative genius. Throughout his travels he always interacted with Armenian intellectuals and worked in Armenian institutions. He also left behind a rich literary legacy. Along with the other slain figures, Taniel Varoujan, Roupen Sevag, Krikor Zohrab and others, he helped raise Western Armenian literature to its apex following a long dormancy only to be cut short by the Genocide. He stands as one of the towering figures of that renaissance. He was 37-years-old when he too was tortured to death a few months after his arrest.

THE DANCE

In a field of cinders where Armenian life was still dying,
a German woman, trying not to cry
told me the horror she witnessed:

"This thing I'm telling you about,
I saw with my own eyes,

Behind my window of hell
I clenched my teeth and watched the town of Bardez turn into a
heap of ashes.
The corpses were piled high as trees,
and from the springs, from the streams and the road,
the blood was a stubborn murmur,
and still calls revenge in my ear.

Don't be afraid; I must tell you what I saw.
so people will understand
the crimes men do to men.
For two days, by the road to the graveyard ...

Let the hearts of the world understand,
It was Sunday morning,
the first useless Sunday dawning on the corpses.
From dawn to dusk I had been in my room
with a stabbed woman —
my tears wetting her death —
when I heard from afar
a dark crowd standing in a vineyard
lashing twenty brides and singing filthy songs.

Leaving the half-dead girl on the straw mattress,
I went to the balcony of my window
and the crowd seemed to thicken like a clump of trees

An animal of a man shouted, "You must dance,
dance when our drum beats."
With fury whips crackedon the flesh of these women.
Hand in hand the brides began their circle dance.
Now, I envied my wounded neighbor
because with a calm snore she cursed
the universe and gave up her soul to the stars ...

"Dance," they raved,
"dance till you die, infidel beauties
With your flapping tits, dance!
Smile for us. You're abandoned now,
you're naked slaves,
so dance like a bunch of fuckin' sluts.
We're hot for your dead bodies.
Twenty graceful brides collapsed.
"Get up," the crowed screamed,
brandishing their swords.

Then someone brought a jug of kerosene.
Human justice, I spit in your face.
The brides were anointed.
"Dance," they thundered —
"here's a fragrance you can't get in Arabia."
With a torch, they set the naked brides on fire.
And the charred bodies rolled and tumbled to their deaths ...

I slammed my shutters,

sat down next to my dead girl

and asked: "How can I dig out my eyes?"

Translated by Peter Balakian and Nevart Yaghlian

20. *Vorbes Hishadag Anmoratsoutian*

(In remembrance of Albert and Vache')

I borrowed the title from the inscription on the back of a picture my late cousin Vache' Apelian had sent me decades earlier from Canada. Those who do not understand its meaning will have to continue on reading to find out what it means.

On a typical early autumn morning day in Beirut, for all certainty in 1967, out of blue, Vache' and Albert Apelian sprang onto the veranda of Hotel Lux, the hotel my father ran. The previous night they had left for good Keurkune, their ancestral village and birthplace, where each could trace his lineage for eight or nine generations.

I had met both of them in Keurkune a year before. It was the first trip I had taken to Keurkune driving the family's first car, a VW Beetle. Vache' and Albert came to visit me not long after I arrived. They were the tail ends of our immediate generation born to Keurkunetsi parents. They were two years younger than I. There was a time when these two years had put us much like North and South poles apart. Time had moved on and I felt towards both a stronger kinship than ever before. They were the remaining two in the village. The rest of our immediate generation had already moved out of the village to carve their courses in life.

Seeing both of them together I realized that both had left behind their childhood rivalaries and seemed to have drawn closer to each other. They had become bosom friends. They took me for a walk through the village and enthusiastically pointed to me the long wooden poles that lay along the side of the main dirt road of the village. I remember very well the ambivalence that overtook me at the sight of these poles. Civilization was encroaching upon our village. Its tentacles were spreading over the coming electric wires. There and then I realized that a way of life I knew was being relegated to the footnotes of history.

Meeting them again on the veranda of Hotel Lux that autumn day morning was a pleasant surprise, to say the least. It turned out that there was more to their coming than a simple visit. Vache' and Alberteg, having reached conscription age, had dodged their upcoming military draft. They had put themselves at the mercy of a local smuggler who had directed them through open fields, shallow waters and had them cross on four legs across railroad tracks spanning over a river into Lebanon. Their clothing attested to their plight the night before.

Almost always more of those born and raised in the village have settled outside the village. Keurkune, much like

greater Kessab, with its limited resources could not possibly sustain its natural growth. Consequently many of its youth always left the villages and ventured out and settled in almost all the continents. The allure of a world far beyond had taken a better hold of their youthful imagination as well. They were excited, restless to cross the Atlantic and they did.

Albert: We never called him by his name but by his endearing nickname - Alberteg. As a sideline note, '-eg' if preceded by a consonant or only 'g' if preceded by a vowel are Armenian suffixes added to a name to make it more endearing, such as Vaheg, instead of Vahe', Alberteg instead of Albert, Vartoug instead of Varthouhie. Albert most probably was named after his paternal uncle Dr. Albert Apelian, a physician and a bilingual prolific writer, who passed away in Massachusetts.

I visited Albert and his mother the night before his departure to bid him farewell. He was staying at a cousin's house. She had come from Keurkune to accompany her son to the airport and bid him farewell. I do not remember if I went to the airport as well. Most likely than not, I did. I never heard from him after he left, although I would hear of him.

I met Albert after I moved to the New World more than two decades later. It so happened that my employer at the time was headquartered in Corona, California where I would frequent on business trips and would make a point of meeting him and his brother Zeron. He had not changed much. His abrupt movements and mannerism and his characteristic walking style had not changed. He still had this untamed free spirit in him, at least the outward semblance of it. If I would draw a metaphor, he reminded me of a mustang on a prairie; untamed, free spirited and adventurous. He had gotten married and fathered children and had grown into much loving and caring father. He had become a very successful car salesman. I imagine that he presented to his customers the attributes of the cars he sold with the same enthused animation he described his hunts to us.

Albert succumbed to his illness and passed away prematurely in the prime of his life. During the last few years of his life he visited Keurkune always in autumn to hunt *soumoun*, the migratory birds that made their passage through Kessab as they had always done every God given fall. Albert loved Keurkune. I doubt that there was another place he cared and loved so much and could have possibly grown to care and love that much.

He had visited Vache' a few months before his death and expressed to him his desire to pen his memoirs. I am sure he had much to write to bridge his day-to-day reality in America with the world he carried with him that essentially remained his to the very end, Keurkune.

Vache'. Not long after Albert left for America, Vache' secured his clearance as well to emigrate to Canada. Papken, who was waiting for his Canadian immigration papers as well and I came together to bid him farewell.

We invited him to a restaurant on the Bay of Jounieh, at outskirts of Beirut, at the foot of the hill that housed the famed Casino Du Liban. The Bay of Jounieh is the most picturesque in greater Beirut. We had mezza, the middle-eastern styled buffet consisting of small portion servings of a large wide variety of food in tens of small plates. Arak, the anis oil flavored Middle Eastern spirit, accompanied the dishes. In my opinion these are best savored in a Middle Eastern restaurant overlooking the Mediterranean Sea and nowhere else. We talked at length. The reflection of the glittering lights of greater Beirut during that night on the calm waters of the bay has remained etched in my memory.

On our return there was not much left for us to talk in the car anymore. All that was needed to be said and be introspective about was said and done. We had known each other since we became conscious of our surroundings. We had spent all of our summers together in Keurkune. We had our own rites of passage from wearing the brick red colored *yemeni* shoes to wearing sandals and carrying our own hunting rifles. We had organized hunting, fishing and exploring expeditions together. We had grazed the family animals together, watered the vegetable gardens, treaded tobacco leaves and made the gluey bird catching sticks together. We were now leaving those carefree summers behind and were on our ways to chart our courses in life. The others of our generation, save Papken, had already crossed both the Atlantic and the Pacific Oceans. Papken was to follow suit. We knew that it would be long in the future, if ever, that we might get together once again. Papken broke the deafening silence in the car with an Armenian song. He sang well. I do not remember if I went to the airport the next day to bid him farewell. More likely than not, I did.

Vache' wrote to me after he moved to Canada. He even sent me pictures of him taken at the Niagara Falls. He looked jubilant. On the back of one of the pictures he hand inscribed the following in Armenian "To Dear Vahe', in remembrance of un-forgetfulness". Better said in Armenian, "Sireli Vahe, Vorbes heshadag anmoratsoutian", dated August 24, 1969. I still have the picture.

Our correspondence came to a mutual and natural end. The next time I met him was more than two decades later when he and his wife Karen visited me at my late brother's house during my visit to Los Angeles. By then Vache' had become a family man. He had married Karen in Canada and both had moved to LA to be close to Vache's extended family.

Outgoing, personable and entrepreneurial, Vache' fared well in the New World. He became a proud father to their four daughters. I visited him in his store whenever I came to

146

Los Angeles. His once thick, smooth, free flowing and charcoal black hair had receded and bore testament of the passage of time. However, he remained his old self,

personable, pleasant, hospitable and genuine. He was fun to socialize with. With an excitement of someone who realizes that time has indeed moved on, he told me during one of such visits that he soon will become a *baboug*, the old fashioned all caring and loving Kessabtsi grandpa. But that was not meant to be. Vache' died prematurely of a massive heart.

Vache' became my only childhood friend from Keurkune with whom I accidentally connected in the cyber world. We reminisced of by the gone days, exchanged news and pleasantries as we played *tavloo* – backgammon - while being 2500 miles away.

I could not attend his funeral but made a point of parting from him for good in another way, maybe telling and fitting of our times. On the day of his funeral I opted to remove his name from my friends' list where I would see his name highlighted alerting me of his availability. Clicking the delete key to remove a friend's name from my contact list for the very first time became the most reflective task I had done on the computer. I have done it since but with the familiarity of someone who, over the course of years, makes peace with the inevitable reality of attending the funerals of family members, relatives and friends and then deleting their names from the cyber contact list.

Before deleting his name, I opened his virtual mail box and typed in English characters, reading Armenian, as we chatted that way, "Asdoutz Hedt" – "Godspeed" and sent the message away and then pressed the delete key and removed his name in an attempt to put a closure to another chapter of the ever unfolding book of our lives.

21 #RebuildKessab

Kessab Center

Kantsasar, the official publication of the Aleppo Prelacy of the Armenian Apostolic Church, reported on June 16, 2014 that the Syrian Arab Army forces had advanced into Kessab and were stationed in the city square. The report effectively heralded the liberation of the mostly Armenian-inhabited Kessab on Fathers' Day.

The following day official Syrian sources reported that some of the residents of Kessab had begun to return from the coastal town of Latakia--where they had taken refuge--to check on their homes, businesses, churches and community centers.

Eighty-eight days earlier, on the morning of March 21, 2014 extremists from Turkey attacked the peaceful inhabitants of Kessab with an onslaught of artillery fire.

Defenseless and on their own, a veritable carnage awaited them had they stayed put. They helped each other evacuate the villages in a matter of few hours and ran for their lives to the coastal city Latakia with no more than their clothes on. From there on until its liberation the greater Kessab remained at the mercy of these extremists.

Upon their return the Kessabtsis found their homes uninhabitable because they were vandalized, looted and burned; their churches desecrated and torched; their businesses, community centers similarly vandalized, looted and torched to different degrees. The orchards left unattended had gone wild with outgrowth. The machinery to tend them had been taken away by the plundering raiders. Even the wooden poles supporting the electric grid over the villages were cut off and their wires removed to sell as scrap metal. The dead were also not spared as some cemeteries were desecrated and graves opened. Turkey had left its borders open for the plundering crowd to haul its loot. My cousin's soap factory was similarly looted bare. Its noted LaurApel brand soaps were reported being sold in Turkey.

In short, over a century long hard work was wiped away in a matter of weeks. The desecrated and torched Armenian Evangelical Holy Martyrs Church that stood in the center of village bore witness to the hard work the native Kessabtsi Armenians had painstakingly vested to make Kessab the tourist magnet it had become before the civil war erupted.

The construction of the Holy Martyrs Church was commenced under the leadership of Rev. Dikran Koundakjian in the aftermath of the 1909 pogrom and sacking of Kessab. The first evangelical church of Kessab, founded in 1853, was destroyed in that carnage. Instead of rebuilding the destroyed church, Rev. Koundakjian spearheaded the building of even a larger and a more elegant church with white to off white stones quarried locally. In popular parlance the church became to be known as the "White Church". The 1915 genocidal deportation began not long after halting its construction. The surviving Kessabtsis who managed to return to their villages in 1918 were too poor to undertake its completion. The church stood as bare four walls in the center of the Kessab, open to the elements of nature. It would take some 60 years for the Kessabtsis to put a roof on the four walls. Under the leadership of Rev. Ardashes Kerbabian, sometime early 1970's, the construction of the church was completed. The church was overhauled and renovated in the early 1990's. The church they had cared so much, they found mercilessly torched and desecrated along with much of the greater Kessab.

Missakian Cultural Center

At the location of the old church, across the Holy Martyrs Church and next to the Armenian Evangelical School, a charming cultural center was erected and named after its benefactor as Missakian Cultural Center. It was completely burned down and was still smoldering when the Kessabtis returned to check on their villages.

What the visitors to Kessab saw and experienced bore a stark resemblance to what Miss. Effie Chambers, their beloved American missionary, witnessed in the aftermath of the 1909 sack and pogrom of the greater Kessab. "It was a most desolate picture that greeted my eyes," she wrote in her unpublished autobiography her family has shared with me. 'Houses had been burned after being looted, and silk worm eggs in the hatching process (one of the principal financial resources of the region) had been destroyed. The gardens stood in ruins. The grapevines, and other foods used for standby winter diets, such as raisins and molasses, were damaged beyond hope. The houses, my own, the Mission House, Girls' School, church, parsonage, and the market were all a holocaust. The outside villages fared the same."

The plight of the Kessabtsis in the aftermath of the March 21, 2014 attack caught the attention of the world primarily thanks to a cadre of young Armenian-Americans, savvy in the new communication modes. They made effective use of social media. Kim Kardashian, who commands over twenty million followers on Twitter, joined in trending the "#SaveKessab" hashtag. Right after the liberation of Kessab, a new hashtag appeared on the social media - "#RebuildKessab" - signaling the rebuilding of Kessab. It is the sheer tenacity of the native inhabitants that made their continuous habitation in that desolate and rugged mountainous terrain over the past many centuries possible.

Father Nareg Louisian

Upon his return on the very day of the liberation, Father Nareg Louisian reported having rendered service at the vandalized gravesite of the Armenian Catholic priests buried in the church compound. On July 16, 2014 he reported on his Facebook page that the St. Michael Armenian Catholic Church was cleaned of rubble and debris, thanks to the diligence of its parishioners and was ready for Holy Mass. The Saint Michael Church, much like the other churches, had been desecrated and vandalized but it had not been torched. Father Nareg invited the clergy and the members of the other two denominations to use their sanctuary, saying that St. Michaels' Church is their sanctuary as well.

`On July 05, 2014 Rev. Haroutune George Selimian, the president of the Armenian Evangelical Community in Syria, paid an official visit to Kessab accompanied by an official delegation from Latakia. Rev. Sevag Trashian, the pastor of the Armenian

Rev. Haroutune Selimian

Evangelical Church of Kessab, and lay dignitaries from Kessab met him and toured the evangelical churches of Kessab and its villages Keurkune, Ekizolouk, Karadouran. All were vandalized to varying degrees but the churches in Kessab and Keurkune were torched and burned all through.

Rev. Sevag Trashian

Rev. Selimian launched the cleaning and the restoration of the Evangelical churches by symbolically wiping away slogans written by the extremists on the walls of the Holy Martyrs Church. He also addressed in Arabic the people and the members of the press covering his visit. He said that Armenians stand firm on their land in Kessab and remain faithful citizens of the Syrian Arab Republic. The Syrian officials, in turn, promised to provide Kessab with the necessities to re-establish power and water supply. The restoration work of the Armenian Evangelical churches in greater Kessab thus began.

Arch. Shahan Sarkissian

On Friday July 25, 2014 Archbishop Shahan Sarkissian, the prelate of the Aleppo Armenian Apostolic Prelacy, consecrated the desecrated Armenian Apostolic Church of Kaladouran, Kessab's coastal village. Lay and clergy representatives from the other two denominations attended the consecration. Next evening divine service was conducted and on Sunday Holy Mass was held for the first time in the newly consecrated church.

Historians will have to ascertain these dates given that their reporting on Facebook pages may not have happened on the very same day these events took place.

Miss Effie Chambers had gone to Adana to assist the survivors of one of the worst atrocities perpetrated against the Armenians in Turkey when marauding Turkish mobs attacked Kessab on the morning of April 23, 1909. She wrote in her autobiography: 'Upon my arrival [to Kessab] the people, those who could get around, were assembled in the yard of the Mission House to greet me."

'Their first question was 'Will you stay with us and help us start again?'

I said: 'That is what I came for, to stay and help you get on your feet again. If you want to stay we'll do it and God will help us rebuild our homes, shops, and churches and reclaim your land.'

'Is it a promise?' they asked.

I said: 'Yes, on my part it is.'

'On ours also,' was the reply.

"I can't tell you how we did it." She elaborated further. "Just step by step, one day at a time, and by the autumn of 1911, before the rains set in, those who had stayed in Kessab and lived through the horrible ordeal, were back in their rebuilt houses, with their schools and churches going."

President Serzh Sarkissian of Armenia characterized this latest tragedy as the third expulsion of the people from

Kessab in reference to the 1909 porgrom and sacking of the villages and the 1915 Genocide.

At the aftermath of the latest expulsion, an uphill struggle awaits the native inhabitants to piece together their shattered lives anew and to rebuild Kessab once more.

22. Խաչակիրը

Շաբաթ 18 Հոկտեմբեր 2008։
Աբելեաններուն տոհմիկ գիւղէն -
Քէոբքիւնայէն - շատ շատ հեռու, զոյգ
քաղաքներ (Twin Cities) կոչուած
քաղաքին օրակայանին մէջն էի, երբ
հեռաձայնով մայրս գուժեց ծործ
Աբելեանին (ՕՆ.1945) վաղաճամ
մահուան լուրը։ Մահը պատահած էր
այդ Շաբաթ օրուան վաղ առաւօտեան
ժամերուն եւ մարմինը ամփոփուած էր

Քէոբքիւնայի պապենական գերեզմանատան մէջ նոյն օրը, կէսօրէ եսմ՝
յետ արարողութեան Քէոբքիւնայի պատմական Հայ Աւետարանական
եկեղեցւոյ մէջ։ Չէի կրնար պատկերացնել աւելի պատշաճ եւ ծորբը

ամբողջացնող հանգստեան վերջին կայան մը անողոք հիւանդութեան մէջ մաշած իր մարմինին համար: Կարծես ինքն ալ անոր համար կատարած էր իր վերջին ուղեւորութիւնը դէպի իր արմատները: Խաբուսիկ բայց հանգստացնող բան մը ունի ծործի թաղման այս իրողութիւնը:

Սպասման սրահին մէջ²ն եմ դէպի Լոս Անճելոս ուղեւորութեան համար, ուր այնպայմանօրէն կը հանդիպեի իրեն: Բնականաբար կը պրպտեմ յիշողութիւնս եւ հոն կը գտնեմ զինէ ոչ որպէս առօրեայ ներկայութիւն, այլ մեր կեանքին հանգրուաններուն շարանին մէջ: Քէօրքիւնայի մէջն է ան, երբ մենք տակաւին պատանիներ կը խաղայինք իրենց ընտանիքին պատկանող Նոֆերենց հոչակաւոր մանկանային – ձիթհանին - շուրջ: Աւիլի ուշ, Հալէպի մէջ, երբ ես որպէս սկաուտ Պէյրութէն կը մասնակցէի ՀՄԸՄ մարզական խաղերու տողանցքին, կը հանդիպէի ծործին: Տարիներ վերջ Պէյրութ եմ ուսանողական մեր տարիներուն, ուր արդէն ցոյց կու տար կուտակուած ազգասիրութեան մը իրայատուկ եռանդ: Եւ վերջապէս Լոս Անճելոս է եւ տակաւին պատանէ¹ի վրայ` իբր հեռատեսելի "Դիրքերու Հետ" շաբաթական յայտագիրով, որ վարեց տասնամեակ մը` պատգամելով իր եղէգնեայ գրիչով:

Այսպէս ծործը բնակեցաւ Քեսապ, Հալէպ, Պէյրութ, Լոս Անճելոս; բայց միշտ ապրեցաւ բիւրեղացած իր հայ ներաշխարհէն ներս: Չեմ գիտեր բնութեան n°ր դասաւորումը այսքան հայքինասիրութին կուտակած էր այս տողուն հոգիէն ներս, չրսելու համար հայրենապաշտութեամբ բեռնաւորած էր զինէ, որպէս խաչ մը, որ տառացիօրէն ուսամբարձ շալկեց Ապրիլ 24-ին, 1972-ի հաւաքական հեռիտոտն ուխտագնացութեան ընթացքին, Անթիլիասի վանքէն դէպի Պիֆֆայայի բարձունքին վրայ գտնող Մեծ

Եղեռնի յուշարձանը: Հայաստանի անկախութենէն եամ կրկին անգամ կատարեց խաչակրութիւն մը դէպի Գարիգին Նժդեհի շիրիմը որպէս ուխտագրացութիւն:

Ծործը չկրցաւ տեսնել ազգային տոհմիկ արժէքներով բիւրեղացած հայախմբումի իրողութիւնը իր պատմական հողերուն վրայ: Սակայն բախտաւորութիւնը ունեցաւ ապրիլ անոր անհատական եւ մտերմիկ իրողութիւնը, յանձին Հալէպի մէջ ծնած, հայկական տոհմիկ ընտանիքի մէջ հասակ առած, Շաֆէ անունով հայ աղջկայ մը մօտ, որ դարձաւ Ծործի կեանքին հարազատ եւ անձնուրաց ընկերակիցը մինչեւ վերջ:

Այսպէս, Ծործի բովանդակ կեանքը ազգային հաւաֆական իտէալին որոնումը եղաւ որպէս տանար մը կառուցուած անխարդախ արժէքներու վրայ, ուր կմախֆացած հայորդիներ պիտի հաղորդուէին այդ իտէալներով, վերակենդանանալու համար: Կ'ուզեմ հաւատալ որ այդ ձգտումին գնահատանֆը ապրեցաւ իր վերջին տարին: Կը հաւատամ այդ եղաւ այն պահուն, երբ, հեռատեսիլի կայանի վրայ, հայ երիտասարդ եւ երիտասարդուհի մը գինֆ հրաւիրեցին ըլլալ, հայ երիտասարդութեան պատգամաբերը 2008-ի Ապրիլ 24-ի առթիւ ֆաղաֆական հաւաֆին, իրեն յանձնելով գնահատագրի տախտակ մը:

Ես մեր իրողութեան մէջ չեմ հանդիպած նման ինքնարուխ զնահատանքի, այդ ալ հայ երիտասարդութեան կողմէ, մեկու մը, որ ո՛չ ուսուցիչ է, ո՛չ կրոնական կամ կուսակցական, եւ հետեւաբար չի պատկանիր որեւէ միութեան մը՝ ըլլայ այդ կրթական, մշակութային, կրոնական կամ թաղական։ Ան ինքնատիպ անձ մըն է իր ուրոյն համոզումներով, անսակարկ ազգասիրութեամբ մը տոգորուած եւ բացարձակապէս խիզախ։

Մահուրնէ քանի մը ամիսներ առաջ իր շրջապատը զուարթացնելու տրամադրութեամբ այսպէս արտահայտուեցաւ. «Ես արդէն անդի աշխարհին հետ կապի մէջ եմ, ամէնեն ալ հոն են։ Հետեւաբար այս ազգին մագին անգամ դպչողը թող չկարծէ որ ինձմէ ազատած է»։

Կեանքին եւ գործին կառչած այս տղուն հրամայականը ազգասիրութիւնն էր ամէն բանէ առաջ եւ ամէն բանէ վեր։ Այդպէս ալ տառացիօրէն մնաց մինչեւ իր մահուան սեմին, ինչպէս կը վկայէն իր կինը Շաքէն եւ եղբայրը Աշոտը։ Երբ ան մահուան սեմին էր եւ ուժասպառ, գերմարդկային ճիգով մը Քէսապէն շուրջ 100 բիլումէրբ անդին, արաբացած եւ իսլամացած զիլդ մը զնաց զգաստութեան բերելու համար զիւղացիները իրենց հայ տոհմիկ ժառանգութեան։

Սիրելի եւ աննոռանալի Ճորճ։ Ահաւասիկ հինգ տարիներ անցած են վաղամեռ մահուանդ վրայ։ Այժմ դուն շրջապատուած ես քու հարազատներովդ եւ պատսպարուած Քէորքիւնայի դարաւոր կաղնիին հովանիին տակ որպէս յիշատակ։ Պիտի չզարմանամ որ գերեզմանդ ուխտատեղի մը դառնայ եղեգնեայ գրիչը ձեռքիդ պատգամներուդ ականջալուր Արմէնին եւ Արմէնուհիին, որոնք տարիներու ընթացքին ալեւորած եւ ալեհեր, այցելեն շիրիմիդ՝ հաղորդուելու համար, որ ազգային իտէալները կարելի է թարմ պահել ամբողջ կեանքի մը տեւողութեան, ինչպէս դուն ըրիր քու բովանդակ կեանքիդ ընթացքին:

23. Սպաղանաց Մակար

Պատանեկան տարիքս դեռ նոր թեւակոխած էի երբ հայրս զիս անդամագրեց Պէյրութի Հ.Յ.Դ. Բարգէն Սինի Պատանեկան Միութեան որուն հանդիպումները տեղի կ՚ունենային «Ժողովրդային Տան» մէջ, հնադարեան ու հնամաշ շէնքէ մը ներս։ Ժողովասրահի պատերուն վրայի նկարները, անոր մնայուն բնակիչ Շապազ Հայրիկը, սենեակները

օգտագործող երիտասարդները եւ տարեց մարդիկը, խորհրդաւոր մթնոլորտ մը կը ստեղծէին կառոյցով խախուտ այդ ժողովասրահէն ներս։

167

Այս մթնոլորտին մէջ էր, որ կը սկսէր Բարգէն Սիւնի Պատանեկան Միութեան ազգային դաստիարակութիւնը, որուն տարեկան հերթականութեամբ, անպայմանօրէն մաս կը կազմէր Բարգէն Սիւնին, Պանֆ Օրոմանի Գրաւումը եւ Սպաղանաց Մակարի Դէպքը: Ժամանակի ընթացքին դէպքերը եւ դէմքերը որոնց իրավիճակ կը ստանային մեր պատանեկան մտաշխարհներուն մէջ շնորհիւ լուսանկարներուն, բայց Սպաղանաց Մակարի պարագան տարբեր էր: Ան որեւէ նկար չունէր: Ո՛չ պատերուն վրայ, եւ ո՛չ ալ գիրքերուն մէջ:

Հ. Յ. Դ. Հարիւրամեակի Յուշամատեանը թղթատած միջոցիս, հանդիպեցայ Սպաղանաց Մակարի համար յարմարցուած, գծագրուած դիմանկարի մը, որ գետեղուած էր Գէորգ Չաւուշի լուսանկարին կողքին: Պատուան լուսանկար մըն է անկասկած, երբեմնի Սասնայ Սպղանֆի իշխան Մակարին, որ պատանեկան օրերէս ի վեր իմ մէջս մնացած է Sօրf Անգեղի նման տարտամ մտապատկեր մը:

Սպաղանաց Մակարի եւ Գէորգ Չաւուշի տարակարծութեան պատճառը, ինչպէս Ռուբէն Փաշան կը ներկայացնէ իր յուշերուն մէջ, Գէորգ Չաւուշի ամուսնութիւնն էր: Կրնայ ըլլալ որ այլ պատճառներ ալ կային: Վերջին հաշուով հայդուկապետին եւ իր զինակիցներուն միջեւ անկասկած որ տարակարծութիւններ կը ծագէին, որոնֆ շատ հաւանաբար կը հարթուէին տեղւոյն վրայ: Բայց այս պարագան տարբեր էր:

Գէորգ Չաւուշ հայդուկապետն էր, սակայն իրեն տարակարծիֆ զինակիցը` Սպաղանաց Մակար, պարզ ֆետտայի մը չէր: Սպաղանաց Մակարի վարկն ու հեղինակութիւնը այնֆա՛ն ազդեցիկ էր, որ Հ. Յ. Դ.եան Գերագոյն մարմինը մասնաւոր պատուիրակ կը ղրկեր, յանձինս Ռուբէն

Տէր Մինասեանի, հարթելու համար այս երկու հեղինակաւոր հայդուկներուն միջեւ ծագած տարակարծութիւնը, որ սկսած էր վնասել ֆետայական աշխատանքներուն։ Թէ ինչպէս Ռուբէն տնօրինեց պարագան, այդ կը թողում ընթերցողին հետաքրքրութեան։ Այս դէպքը հոս կը ներկայացնեմ բնորոշելու համար Սապաղանց Մակարի հեղինակութիւնը, որ ո՛չ միայն կը տարածուէր Դուրան Բարձրաւանդակին վրայ, այլ կը հասնէր մինչեւ Հ. Յ. Դ.եան Գերագոյն մարմինը։

Ո՞վ էր Սապաղանց Մակարը

Սապաղանց Մակարը Սասնայ Սպդանֆի տէրն ու իշխանն էր։ Ռուբէն իր յուշերուն մէջ կը նկարագրէ զինք որպէս «Աժդահա մը, շա՛տ ապարկու»։ Ժողովուրդը կ՚ըսէր, «Գէորգ գայլ է կամ վագր, իսկ ֆեռի Մակարն էլ, կռուի ժամանակ զարկած գումէc է»։ Եւ իրաւ կը յուcէ Ռուբէն, «Մեծ ու արիւնոտ աչքերով, խոշոր զլխով եւ հսկայ մարմինով այդ աժդահա մարդը, կռուի

ժամանակ ո՛չ աջ կը նայէր, եւ ո՛չ ալ ձախ. ապարկու ձայնով, խենշարը ձեռքին առաջ կ՚երթար եւ կամ անշարժ կը մնար, թէկուզ հարիւրաւոր ընդանօրէններ պայթէին իր վրայ»։

Սասնայ լեռներուն վրայ ծնած ու հասակ առած այս մարդը, բնութեան անդադար զաւակը եղած ըլլալու էր: Անուս, անգրագէտ եւ առհասարակ ո՛չ մէկ կարիքը զգացած ըլլալու էր ո՛չ մէկ խորամանկութեան կամ որեւէ փափկանկատութեան: Աւատապետի իր հանգամանքով բիրտ էր ու ըմբոստ: «Ունումով մարդիկ բրնց Տամատեան, բրնց Գուրգէն, Արմէնակ, վեր մերին զլխուն զլխաւո՞ր...: Իդա ի՞նչ է Արապո եւ Մուրատ, հա Ապրոն ու Գէորգ, թեկուզ իմ սանահէր Սերոբ: Զրմէնն ալ բրնց Մակար չարժէն»: Սպաղանաց Իշխան Մակարի համար ամէնքը առաւելագոյն պարագային իրեն գործակիցներ էին:

Ե՞րբ եւ ինչո՞ւ Սպաղանաց Մակարը անդամակցած է ֆէտային

Սպաղանաց Մակարը ֆէտային անդամակցելով, հաւատարիմ մնացած էր ֆէտայական աւանդական կարգ ու սարքին եւ չէր կազմած իր սեփական ընտանիքը: Երեւոյթները ցոյց կու տան որ ան ֆէտային անդամակցած էր, երբ հայդուկային շարժումը սկսած էր կազմակերպչական բնոյթ ստանալ Դուրան Բարձրավանդակէն ներս: Ան դարձած էր զինակիցը Սերոբ Աղբիւրի, Գէորգ Չաւուշի, Հրայրի, Անդրանիկի, Մուրատի, Տամատեանի եւ Տարոնի այլ անուանի ֆէտայիններուն, որոնք գործեցին Սասունի եւ Տարոնի Բարձրավանդակէն ներս: Իր զինակիցները արժանացան զէք լուսանկարի մը, ինչպէս է պարագամ Գէորգ Չաւուշի, լուսանկարուած Աղբամար կղզիի ժայռերուն վրայ՝ Վահան Փափազեանին կողմէ: Սակայն հայդուկային կեանքը զրկեց Սպաղանաց Մակարը այդ պերճանքէն իսկ: Եւ ան պատանի երեւակայութեանս մէջ մնաց Զէնով Օհանին եւ Տորք Անգեղին նման մտապատկեր մը:

Սպադանաց Մակարի ֆէտայի անդամակցութեան դրդապատճառը կարելի է գտնել Մակարի գինակից եւ օր մըն ալ միասնաբար զոհուելու նախատագրուած Շէնիկի Մանուկին եւ Ռուբէն Տէր Մինասեանի միջեւ տեղի ունեցած հետեւեալ խորհրդակցութեան. Ռուբէն հարց տուած էր Շէնիկի Մանուկին, որ Սպադանաց Մակարի նման ունեւոր ընտանիէէ կու գար, թէ ինչո՞ւ ձգած էր իր հողերն ու հանգիստ կեանքը եւ դարձած ֆէտայի:

«Երբ Մարաթուկ կամ Սուրբ Կարապետ ուխտի գնան», կը պատասխանէ Շէնիկ Մանուկ, «մատաղցուի համար չեն ընտրեր կոստա այծերին, անընդունելի է Սուրբին համար, միշտ պէտք է ընտրել զլաւ խոյերին ուխտի նպատակին հասնելու համար: Մեր Աստուած Հայոց ազատութիւնն է, աշիր ու հարուստ հայեր ամէնէն առաջ պէտք է մատուցուին այդ զոհասեղանին»:

Շատ հաւանաբար, նոյն այս հոգեբանութիւնն էր, որ մղած էր Սպադանի աւատապետ Իշխան Մակարը թողնելու իր ընկերային դիրքը, տունը, կալուածները եւ դառնալ ֆէտայի, որուն համար Շէնիկի Մանուկ եւ Սպադանաց Մակար պիտի դառնային պարարտ գոհեր:

Ի՞նչ կռիւներու մասնակցած է Սպադանաց Մակար

Համառոտ կերպով հետեւեալ նախատամարտները կարելի է թուել որոնց մասնակցած էր Սպադանաց Մակար.

- Սերոբ Աղբիւրին դաւադրաբար թունաւորող մարդուն եւ անոր ընտանիէին ահաբեկումը կազմակերպած Անդրանիկի ղեկավարութեամբ:

171

- Պշարէ Խալիլ էիւրտ աշիրէթապետին Սպաղանֆի վրայ յարձակման կռիւը:

- Նոյն այդ Պշարէ Խալիլի գլխատման կռիւը` Անդրանիկի դեկավարու-թեամբ:

- 1890-93 Սասնոյ, Տալւորիկի, Անտոկի, Մշվասրի կռիւները:

- 1904 Սասնայ երկրորդ ապատամբութեան մասնակցութիւնը:

- 1904-08, Տարոնի եւ Վասպուրականի կռիւներուն իր մասնակցութիւնը:

Այս ամբողջ ֆեռայական կռիւներուն, Սպաղանաց Մակար ստացած է հրամանատարի պատասխանատու պարտաւորութիւններ: Շատ հաւանաբար չափազանցութիւն պիտի չըլլայ ճեշտել, որ 1890-էն մինչեւ իր եղերական մահը, Սպաղանաց Մակար մասնակցած է Սասնայ եւ Դուրան Բարձրավանդակի ֆեռայական գլխաւոր

նախատամարտերուն եւ գործած այդ շրջանէն ներս գործող անուանի հայդուկներուն հետ: Սպաղանաց Մակար անգիտակից չէր հայ յեղափոխական շարժման իր բերած նպաստին: Իրեն յատուկ ունով եւ պարզախոսութեամբ, այսպէս կը ներկայացնէր իր բերած նպաստը.

«Ամբողջ հայ ազգը Սասուն կը նայի: Սասունն ալ հայ ազգի հոգին: Իսկ Սասունի հոգին ալ Սպաղանք եղած է: Երբ Սիմալքն Տամատեանը կը մատնէր, երբ Կելիք Կիւզանը Աբոն կը մեղցնէր, երբ ամբողջ դաշտը եւ Վերի Գեալքն Սերոբն ու Գուրգէնը դուրս կը վռնտէին, ո՛վ էր վառ պահեց յեղափոխութեան նրագը, ո՞վ էր որ ֆէտայիններուն օթեւան տուեց եւ կոնակ եղաւ...: Դա՛ Սպաղաննն էր եւ բեռի Մակարը:»

Ի՞նչպէս զոհուեցաւ Սպաղանաց Մակարը

Գէորգ Չաւուշի Սուլուխի նակատամարտին նախատակութեենէն եւմ, Դուրան Բարձրավանդակի մէջ որպէս դեկավարներ մնացին Սպաղանաց Մակարը եւ Ռուբէն Տէր Մինասեանը: Անաւասիկ այն ժամանակ էր որ լուր հասաւ իրենց, որ Գէորգի կինը՝ Եղսն եւ զաւակը՝ Վարդգէս փախնգի մէջ են: Սպաղանաց Մակար ստանձնեց անոնց ապահովութեան պատասխանատուութիւնը: Ան՝ այժմ ստանձնած էր պաշտպանութիւնը կնոջ մը, որուն ամուսնութիւնը իր եւ իր զինակիցին միջեւ խոր տարակարծութեան պատճառ հանդիսացած էր:

Երբեմնի հայդուկապետ Գէորգ Չաւուշի ընտանիքը փոխադրելու ժամանակ, Մակարը պաշարուեցաւ իր զինակից Շենիկի Մանուկին հետ: Մակարը փախցնել տուաւ Գէորգի զաւակը՝ Վարդգէսը, ըսելով որ «ճիծ է, զուցե փրկուի»: Իսկ Գէորգի կինը՝ Եղսն, իր անմիջական պաշտպանութեան տակ պահեց, ըսելով. «Եղսն նամուս է, պետմ չէ բշնամիին ձեռքը անգնի»: Եղսն ու Վարդգէսը փրկուեցան, սակայն

Սպաղանաց Մակարը եւ Շէնիկի Մանուկը դաձան պարարտ խոյերը գոհասեղանին:

ԾԱՆՕԹ. Այս գրութիւնը քաղած եմ ընդհանրապէս մօրեղբօրս՝ Դոկտ. Անդրանիկ Չէլէպեանի «Յեղափոխական Դէմեր» գիրքէն եւ Ռուբէնի «Յուշեր»էն:

Ձուարթ Աբելեան

24. Գաբրիէլը Նափանի Մէջ

Զուարթ Աբէլեանի այս գրութիւնը լոյս տեսաւ **2008-ին** Գաբրիէլ Ինճէնիկեանին ի պատիւ կազմակերպուած հանդիսութեան մը առիթով՝ կազմակերպուած Գալիֆորնիոյ առաջին հայկական միջնակարգ ուսումնական հաստատութեան **Սրբոց Նահատակաց Ֆերահեան Երկրորդական Վարժարանի** շրջանաւարտներուն կողմէ:

Ցորելեարը հիմնադիր տնօրէնն էր դպրոցին *(1964)*, եւ իր անխոնջ աշխատանքներուն շնորհիւ հաստատութիւնը անեցաւ ու ընդարձակուեցաւ հակառակ բազմապիսի դժուարութիւններու՝ յուսադրելով ու մղելով հանրութիւնը նմանօրինակ ազգանուէր աշխատանքներու։ Նոյն վարժարանին մէջ Տիկին Արեւ եան շրջան մը պատունիկը եղած էր Գաբրիէլ Ինենեիկեանին։ .

Այն օրերուն Թեսապը սոսկ զաւառ մրն էր, ու զաւառի պարգ, անպանոյն լեզուով հաղորդուող տղայ մրն էր Գաբին։ Պատահական ռեւէ անհատի հետ հարազատ ազգականի նման խօսելու յատկութիւնը ունէր։ Թեսապի ու համայն շրջաններու միակ բժիշկ, Տոքթոր Աւետիսի Ինենեիկեանին տղան էր։ Դժուար թէ մէկը համարձակէր իրեն պարոն Գաբրիէլ ըսել։ «Մօ՛, այդ "պարոնը" ուրկէ՞ եկաւ. "Շպէն" (թեսապերէն) ընկեր ըսե՛, վերջացաւ»։ Այդպէս ալ մնաց միշտ, համեստ ու ամէնուն բարեկամը։

Եղաւ շրջան մը որ զանազան երկիրներէ ու վարժարաններէ միախումբ դասատուներ Հայաստան հրաւիրուեցան, ինչ որ ուսումնական վերապատրաստման ծրագիրներու հաղորդ դառնալու համար։ Լիբանանի որոշ վարժարաններ ալ օգտուեցան վերոյիշեալ ծրագրումներէն։ Հայ Աւետարանական վարժարանները հրաւէր չստացան։

1970 թուին անձնապէս ռուսական դեսպանատուն գացի։

«Ի՞նչ հարց ունէք, խնդրեմ», հարցուց պարոն մը խիստ կենգադավարի։

«Կը փափաքիմ Պրն. Յակոբեանը տեսնել» (ամէն կարգի հարցերու պատասխանատուն):

«Մի վայրկեան», ըսաւ երիտասարդը ու հանդեպակաց դռնէն ներս մտաւ: Շտապ դուրս գալով «Հրամեցէք, Տիկին», ըսաւ ու հանդիպակաց դուռը ցոյց տուաւ:

Հազիւ ներս մտած`

«Ի՞նչ հարց ունէք, Տիկին», հարցուց ու հրաւիրեց որ նստիմ: Ապա`

«Պարոն Յակոբեան» ըսի, «Պէյրութի մէջ շատ վարժարաններէն ուսուցիչներ Հայաստան դրկուեցան, իսկ մեր վարժարանէն մէկը չգնաց, արդեօք ինչո՞ւ...: Մենք ունինք շուրջ 1000 աշակերտ ու 70-ի շուրջ դասատուներ»:

«Ճիշտը` չգիտեմ, իսկ դո՞ւք ալ դասատու էք հայկական նիւթերի»:

«Այո՛, Պրն Յակոբեան, սակայն ինձմէ անջատ այլ դասատուներ ալ կան նոյն նիւթերով գրաղող»:

Լռեց: Ապա`

«Ինչ էլ լինի պարագան, եթէ նոյնիսկ մէկ վիզա ստանանք` էդ վիզայով դուք պիտի գնաք, վստահ եղէք»:

Այդպէսով, անձնապէս խումբին միանալով գացի Հայաստան: Ամերիկայէն Գաբին ալ մեզի միացաւ Երեւան:

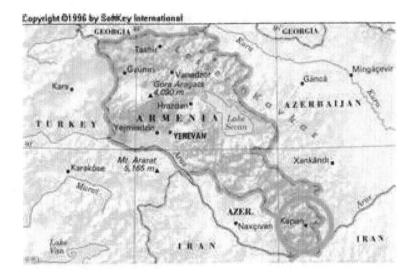

Հայաստանի մէջ հորաֆրոսս աղջկան ընտանիքը կը բնակէր Լափանի շրջան. ընտանիքին մինուճար որդին կը գործէր օդանաւին մէջ, Երեւանէն Լափան գբոսաշրջիկներ տանելու ու վերադարձնելու գործով։ Ամէն պարագայի, մեզի համար արգիլուած շրջան մըն էր այդ։ Հորաֆրոս մանչը յատկապէս եկաւ զիս հոն տանելու։

«Կը ցաւիմ, տղաս, չեմ կրնար երթալ, մեզի համար արգիլուած շրջան է», ըսի։

Ճիշդ այդ միջոցին, Գաբին վերէն վար կ՚իջնէր, երբ իմացաւ թէ հարցը ինչումն է՝

«Տղա՛ս, ես ալ ուսուցիչ եմ, բեսապցի եմ, Ջուարթին ալ ազգական եմ։ Իֆ չ՚երթար, ե՛ս կ՚երթամ, զիս կը տանի՞ս... »

«Շա՛տ լաւ», ըսաւ երիտասարդը։

Հինգ վայրկեանը բաւեց Գաբիին. 2 շապիկ, մէկ ժագէթ ու զիշերպազգեստ մը շալկած վար

իջնելն ու անհետանալը մէկ եղաւ տղուն հետ:

Երկու օր եւ, երեկոյեան, պանդոկ կը մտնէ, հազիւ թէ անկողինին վրայ ընկողմանած՝ հեռախոսը կը ձայնէ.

«Գաբրիէլ ջա՛ն, լաւ ժամանակ անցկացրի՞ր...» Եւ՝ լռութին... Լսելու համար՝ իրենց խօսքով, «Գաբրիէլ ջան, դուք Սովետական Հայաստանում էք գտնւում, մենք տեղեակ ենք Ձեր իրաւանչիր բայլախոխին...»:

Անկասկած որ իրենք գիտէին Գաբիին իրաւանչիր բայլախոխը, սակայն շատ հաւանաբար չէին գիտեր որ իրենց գործը ամէն պարագաներու, ամէն պայմաններու տակ, խիզախ ու յանդուգն մէկու մը հետ էր, որոնք եղան յատկանիշները արտաքնապէս հանդարտ, բայց ներքնապէս աննկուն քեսապցիներուն հարազատ Գաբիին:

25. Խմբային Ասմունքներ

Շա՛տ սիրած եմ «Խմբային Ասմունքները»։ Ջանունք ընկատած են մեծ հեղինակներու կողմէ մեզի ատանդ մնացած գրական գոհարներ։ Անոնք կատարուած են մենասողներու ու խմբական ասմունքողներու կատրողութեամբ։ Խմբային ասմունքները ուսուցանելու են հանդարտօրէն եւ երկար ժամանակամիջոցով, որպէս զի աշակերտներ ընկալեն իմաստը ու սիրելով կատարեն զայն։ Պատահած է որ երկարատեւ ուսուցման միջոցին լրիւ անգիր սորված ու արտասանած եմ զանոնք։ Հիացում ու զարմանք պատճառելով ունկնդիրներուն: Երջանկութեամբ կը յիշեմ բաժին վերցնող աշակերտներուն արտայայտութիւնները ու իրենց ճիզը ապրումով արտասանելու՝ զիս գոհացնելու համար սոսկ:

Կարգ մը իմբային ասմունքներ կամ արտասանելի գրական արձակ կտորներ, պոեմաներ էին. Կրնան տրուած ըլլալ յապաւումներով: Միտք բանին եղած է զանոնք յարմարցնել ճՆշդ. Կրնան տրուած ըլլալ յապաւումներով: Միտք բանին եղած է զանոնք յարմարցնել ճՆշդ. Կրնան տրուած ըլլալ յապաւումներով: Միտք բանին եղած է զանոնք յարմարցնել ճՆշդ.

Հոս ամբարուած բոլոր իմբային ասմունքները իրենց տարբերակներով, վստահաբար օգտագործուած են այս կամ այն վարժարանէն ներս՝ կատարողութեամբ նախակրթարանի կամ երկրորդական բաժնի աւարտական կարգերուն կողմէ եւ կամ զեղարուեստական յայտագիրներու միջոցին, յարմարագոյն դասարանի մը կողմէ:

Ջանունք ձեռք ձգած եմ սովորաբար Անգլիաս դպրեվանքի սաներէն, վարդապետներէն, նաեւ կրթական մշակներէ, թերթերէն եւն...: Աւելի ուշ նկատած եմ որ այս թանկագին ասմունքներէն ոմանց հեղինակները կը պակսին: Գտնել, ճշդել, հնարաւոր չեղաւ: ճիշդ այդ պատճառով ուստի՝ կացութիւնը փրկած եմ «Համադրութիւն» գրելով, տրուած ըլլալով որ մէկէ աւելի հեղինակներու գրութիւններէ առնուած ասոյքներ կան հոն:

Արդարեւ՝ երկրորդ հազարամեակէն ի վեր, ձեռագիրը ատիճանաբար տեղի տուաւ: Համակարգիչը անձնանոթ դիմագիծ մը ստեղծեց մեր գրական աշխատանքներու մարգէն ներս, զոր արագորէն որդեգրեց ուսանողը ու անոր դիմաց հարկադրաբար համբացաւ դասատուն:

Անձնապէս այս նկատառումներէն մղուած որոշեցի **47** տարիներու ուսումնակրթական աշխատանքներուս միջոցին կատարած իրագործումներս, որոնք ընդհանրապէս օրինակով մը, եւ կամ լրիւ տետրակով պահ դրուած էին խաւաքարտէ հաստատուն արկղի մը մէջ, ձեռագիր արտագրել զանոնք ամենապարզ ձեւով, որպէս զի ընթեռնելի ըլլայ ռեւէ անհատի համար:

Հոս տեղին է ըսել, որ տառեր կան մեր այբենարանին մէջ, զորոնք կարելի է գրել նաեւ ուրիշ տառեր պատկերով: Օրինակ: Թ. եւ f, Գ եւ g, Կ եւ կ, Ն եւ Ս, եւն.:

Ի վերջոյ չեմ կրնար, կամ՝ չեմ ուզեր գիտնալ թէ ի՛նչ նակատագիր պիտի ունենան այս գոհարները, անհարագատ այս ափերուն վրայ կամ այլուր: Եթէ չօգտագործուին, չգնահատուին, չեմ ուզեր երեւակայել մոռցուելու մասին, պիտի անհանգստանայ հոգիս: Ինքս մեծ արժէք տուի ու գնահատեցի զանոնք, սնունդէս աւելի:

ԾԱՆՕԹ. վերոյիշեալ գրութիւնը, տիկին Զուարթ Աբէլեանի քանի մը հատորներու մէջ գեղագրած խմաբական արտասանութիւններու հաւաքածոյին ներածականն է:

26. Դէմfեր, Դէպfեր եւ Ցուcեր

Ո՞վ լսած չէ երբեք «Պուրճ Համուտ»ի մասին։ Հայահոծ, հայաբնակ շրջան մը Պէյրութի հիւսիս-Արեւելեան շրջանին մէջ։ Հայրենիքէն հեռու Հայաստան մը դարձած Պուրճ Համուտը։ Ուրիշ

խօսքով հայակերտումի հնոց մը։ Հոն դարբնուեցաւ ու կերտուեցաւ հայ բանուորն ու կրօնաւորը, ուսուցիչն ու փարոզիչը։ Այլ եւ այլ արհեստներու ու արուեստներու մէջ տաղանդ ցուցաբերող աշկերտն ու աշակերտը։ Ուրիշ խօսքով՝ արտադրեց Պուրճ համունտը – նոյնիսկ դարձաւ անեկտոտ երիտասարդներու շրթներուն վրայ։ Բացատրեմ .-

Երբ վրայ հասաւ Լիբանանի քաղաքական անկայուն օրերը, 70-ական թուականին, Պուրճ Համունտի տղամարդը, երիտասարդն ու տարեցը, հարկադրուեցան զէնf կրել իրենց շրջաններու պաշտպանութեան համար։

Երրեմնի ասակերտը դարձաւ ասկերը ինֆնապաստպանութեան մարզին իր դեկավարին, լֆելով ուսումնառութիւնը։ Ուսման ակնարկումի պարագային երբ հարց դրուէր թէ արդեof այս կամ այնինչ ուսանողը կրցա՞ւ իր B.A.-ն ստանալ ... պատասխանը կըլլար .- այդ չենֆ գիտեր, սակայն գիտենֆ որ ան B.H չատացաւ, այսինֆն Պուրն Համուցցի չեղաւ, չկրցաւ ըլլալ։ Այս էր եւ է Լիբանանի Պուրն Համուտը:

Ես ինֆս ալ համարեայ դարձայ Պուրն Համունցցի, fառորդ դար ծառայելով Պուրն Համունտի Նոր Մարաշ շրջանի մէջ հաստատուած Հայ Աւետարանական – Շամլեան-Թաբիկեան երկրորդական վարժարանէն ներս, որպէս հայ գրականութեան եւ հայոց պատմութեան դասատու։ Բազմաբիւ ծանoթութեանց կոդֆին նանշgայ նաեւ fոյր Նուարդ Տէմիրնեանը:Պուրն Համունտի, Նոր Մարաշ շրջանի մէջ գտնուող Հայ Աւետարանական Եկեղեցւոյ Տիկնանց Միութիւնը՝ եկեղեցւոյ կողֆին գործոն Միութիւն մըն էր, որ հոգեւոր ու ընկերաբարոյական ձեռնարկումներով զօրաւիգ կը կանգնէր եկեղեցապատկան զանազան կարիքներուն:

Վերոյիշեալ Եկեղեցասէր Տիկնանց Միութեան գործոն ու նուիրուած անդամներէն մէկն էր Նուարդ քոյր Տէմիրճեանը: Ջինջ կը կոչէին Նուարդ քոյր, քանզի բրոշական հարազատութիւն կը ցուցաբերէր անխտրաբար ռեւ մէկուն: Հոգեւոր քոյր մըն էր, միշտ պատրաստ օգնութեան ձեռ երկարելու ուր որ իր կարողութինԸ կը ներէր:Աստուածաճնշական խոսքով, իր ծառայասիրութեամբ միշտ մղոն մը աւելի ընթացող նուիրեալ մըն էր ան: Ջգալի ներկայութիւն մըն էր նաեւ Եկեղեցասէր Տիկնանց Միութենէն ներս: Ռեւ գործունէութեան մէջ կամովին ու մեծ նուիրումով օժանդակող մըն էր ան տնտեսապէս թէ բարոյապէս: Իսկապէս հոգեւոր նուիրեալ մը:Վարժարանը եկեղեցոյ ծոցին մէջ ըլլալով, շատ անգամներ Տիկնանց Միութեան ձեռնարկներուն՝ երբ խոսելու կամ գեղարուեստական անմիջական յայտագրով մը մասնակցութիւնս բերելու պատեհութինԸ կը տրուէր ինծի, Նուարդ քոյր Տէմիրճեանը, ժպտադէմ ու հոգեկան մեծ բաւարարութեամբ մը կը դիմաւորէր զիս: Օրին մէկը խիստ մեծ փափաք յայտնեց որ իր տունը երթայի միասին բաժակ մը սուրճ առնելու: Գացի:

Համեստ, շատ համեստ բնակարան մըն էր վարժարանին ու եկեղեցւոյ
բաղին մէջ: Նուարդ բրօշ չորս զաւակներն ալ, մեր ճշդապահ
աշակերտներէն էին: Ճշդապահութեան հարցը այս այցելութեամբ
լուծուեցաւ, տրուած ըլլալով որ վարժարանին շատ մօտիկը կը բնակէին:
Իսկ ինչ էր ուրեմն Նուարդ բրօշ յարատեւ գոհունակ ժպիտը դէմքին վրայ,
համեստ այս բնակարանէն դուրս կը մտածէի, եւ ումպ ումպ ըմբոշխած
սուրճին կողբին այլ գրոյց ալ կը կատարէինf, ընդհանրապէս իր
զաւակներուն ուսումնականէն զինֆ հետաքրքրող հարցերու շուրջ:
Համարձակութիւնս հաւաքելով հարց տուի:-- Տիկին Տէմիրճեան, ինչ°
գործով կը զբաղի ձեր ամուսինը:-- Նկարիչ է: Տեսած ըլլալու էf, կը
պատասխանէ:-- Խանութ ունի°, ու°ր, ինչպէ°ս է գործը:-- Ո՛չ խանութ
չունի, բայց Տէրը կ'օգնէ: Ոտքի վրայ հոս-հոն կը նկարէ, կրկնեց Նուարդ
բոյր անբացատրելի երջանկութեամբ: Ես ծարայ մըն եմ իմ Աստուծոյս,

խաղաղ կը յարէ Նուարդ քոյր: Այդ օրէն մենք աւելի կապուեցանք իրարու, ինչպէս հարազատ քոյրեր:* * *Ժամանակի ընթացքին քոյր Նուարդին ամուսինը Վոսամշապուհ դարձաւ մեր վարժարանին մնայուն եկարիչը: Հանդարտաբարոյ ու անտրտունջ մարդ էր եկարիչ Վոսամշապուհը:-- Ինչպէ՞ս կըլլայ որ առաւօտեան այս ժամուն վարժարանին բակը կ'ըլլաք Պրն. Վոսամշապուհ կը հարցնեմ:-- Էհ, գործերուն ականչ մի կախեր իշտէ որ մրն է կանգնի, կը պատասխանէ:-- Երկու շաբաթ սպասէ Պրն. Վոսամշապուհ: Ասակերտական ձեռնարկ մը կը պատրաստեմ, դեր վերջնոդ ասակերտանները մեծաքիւ են: Դուն ալ եկուր եկարէ: Մութիֆի դրան մօտ սեղան մը կը դնենք, դաղարին հոն նստէ, եկարնները ասակերտաններուն ծախելու համար: Անոնց համար գեղեցիկ յիշատակ պիտի մնայ այդ եկարնները: Ուստի այսպէս, յանախկի մեր ձեռնարկները, եռանդուն կեանք ստեղծեցին վարժարանէն ներս, ուր մեծապէս օգտակար եղաւ Պրն. Վոսամշապուհը:-- Օրերդ միշտ լուսաւոր ըլլան Տիկին Ապէլեան, կը կրկներ յաճախ մեր վարժարանին բարի եկարիչը, Պրն. Վոսամշապուհը:*
* *Տրուած ըլլալով որ պատմոնակոչումի առաջին տարիէն իսկ մաս կը կազմէի հատուցման սնտուկին, որպէս կրթական մշակ, իմ ծառայութեան շրջանը իր լրումին հասաւ, Լիբանանի Կրթական Հատուցման Գրասենեակի սահմանումով: Այդ առթիւ հոգաբարձական մարմինը որոշած էր իմ քան հինգ տարիներու ծառայութեանս առիթով զիս պարգեւատրել Հայոց Տիգրան Արքայի ոսկեայ շխանշանով:Ներիխկելալ` սրտի պարտք կը զգամ ըսել, որ շմադրումի ձեռնարկումի ասխատանքներուն կողւանը հանդիսացող Տիար Աբրահամ Թորոսեանին շնորհապարտ եմ: Ամէն անգամ որ առիթը ընծայուի իսօք առնելու այդ ուղղութեամբ,

երախտագիտութեամբ կը յիշեմ իր անունը, ինչպէս նաեւ Տիկինը եւ զաւակները՝ Ռաֆֆին եւ Լեւան, որոնք նոյնպէս մեր աշակերտներն էին: Պարզեւատրումը տեղի ունեցաւ Կիրակի առաւոտ մը Եկեղեցւոյ սրահին մէջ: Մեր նկարիչը այդ առիթով զիս նկարեր ու ապա նկարը մեծցուցեր, շրջանակի մէջ առնելով ու մակագրեր է ինծի նուիրելու համար:Իժբախտաբար մեր բարի նկարիչին կեանքի թելը կտրուեցաւ անժամանակ: Իմ նկարներս որոնց մասին նոյնիսկ իր կողակից Նուարդ քոյրը տեղեակ եղած չէր, ինծի յանձնեց արցունքոտ աչքերով, երբ վշտակցութեան համար տունը այցելեցի: Մինչեւ օրս ալ զուրգզուրանֆով կը պահեմ այդ նկարները, միշտ յիշելով Պուրճ Համուտի մեր վարժարանին նուիրեալ նկարիչ՝ Վռամշապուհն ու իր կողակից՝ քոյր Նուարդ Տէմիրճեաննները:Հազիւ անակնկալ մահուան դառնագոյն վիշտը սպանալու վրայ էր, երբ անսպասելիորէն Լիբանանի քաղաքական առօրեան խանգարուեցաւ: Մեծապէս ցնցեց Լիբանանցի ժողովուրդը տնտեսապէս՝ եւ բարոյապէս: Վաղուայ անորոշութիւնը պատճառ դառաւ ժողովուրդին մեծ մասին փաղաքարող ըլլալուն:Լիբանանի քաղաքացիական պատերազմը տեղական ըլալ նաեւ քոյր Նուարդ Տէմիրճեանի ընտանիքը: Ալ զինֆ տեսնելու պատեհութիւնը չունեցայ: Վստահ եմ որ ան արմատական եղած ծաղիկի մը նմանեցաւ որ, հակառակ բոլոր ջանֆերուն ու ջրտուֆին, չի տոկար օտար հողին ու տակաւ կը թառամի:Երանելի են այն մեռալները որոնֆ Տիրոջմով կը ննջեն. Անոնց անիւնը իր հանգիտը կը գտնէ հողին ներֆեւ, իսկ հոգին իր Տէրը փառաբանելու վայելֆը կ՚ունենայ յաւիտենականութեան մէջ:Նուարդ քոյր «Բարի պատերազմը

192

պատերազմեցաւ, ընթացքը կատարեց եւ հաւատքը պահեց:» (Բ. Տիմ. 4:7)

Օրինեալ ըլլայ իր յիշատակը:

27. Cover Picture Captions

Row 1, Left to Right

1. A portrait of the author, Vahe H. Apelian.

2. A picture of poet Taniel Varoujan on a Republic of Armenia stamp.

3. David Krikorian publicizing the recognition of the Armenian Genocide in Ohio in a press conference on April 24, 2007 in downtown Cincinnati at its famed Fountain Square. The billboard behind, whose message is not visible in the picture, was financed by David and carried the following announcement: "Governor Strickland Proclamation - April 24, 2007 - Armenian Genocide - Ohio Day of Remembrance".

4. Sipan, the second highest mountain of Armenia.

5. Statue of David of Sassoun in Armenia.

Row 2, Left to Right

1. A picture of the Armenian American Pulitzer winning author William Saroyan on a United States postal stamp.
2. Ancient stone carving found in the town Eregli, in the province of Konya, Turkey. The author's father-in-law was born there.
3. The dust cover of the book *Interned in Turkey 1914-1918* by Henry W. Glockler.
4. A portrait of musicologist Bedros Alahaydoyan.
5. A picture of Roupen Sevag on a Republic of Armenia stamp.

Row 3, Left to Right

1. Emblem of the Holy Martyrs Ferrahian Armenian High School, the first Armenian all day school in The United States founded in 1964 by Gabriel Injejikian.

2. The cover of the translated book of Shahan Shahnour's famous novel.

3. A picture of silkworms on mulberry leaves.

4. A portrait of the late Vache' Apelian.

5. A scene from the recess period of the students of Shamlian Tatikian Armenian Evangelical High School in Bourj Hamoud, Lebanon. Pictured by Mrs. Zvart Apelian.

Row 4, Left to Right

1. A picture of Hagop Martayan-Dilaçar's tombstone by Hrach Kalsahakian (www.azad-hye.net).

2. A portrait of Mrs. Zvart Apelian.

3. A portrait of Mr. Gabriel Injejikian, the founding principal of the first Armenian school in The United States of America.

4. A scene from the overwhelmingly Armenian inhabited town Bourj Hammoud in Lebanon.

5. A common presentation of the hashtag #RebuildKessab on social media.

Vahe H. Apelian is born in Beirut. He received his primary and middle school level education at the Sourp (Saint) Nshan, presently Souren Khanamirian Armenian National School and his high school education at the Armenian Evangelical College presently the Yeprem and Martha Philibosian Armenian Evangelical College. He continued his education at the American University of Beirut where he received Sophomore Diploma in Arts and Sciences, B.S. in Pharmacy and M.S. in microbiology. Subsequently he was accepted as a fellow to be trained as a clinical pathologist at the American University Hospital. After immigrating to The United States in 1976, Vahe's career of over three decades spanned in the development of drug delivery systems with multinational pharmaceutical companies where he held scientific and managerial positions. He furthered his education while employed and received his second M.S. degree in Industrial Pharmaceutical Sciences and PhD in Pharmaceutics from St. John's University in New York. In recognition of his academic excellence, he is elected to Rho Chi, the only national Pharmaceutical Honors Society. Vahe has published, presented and co-authored in his line of specialty. He is the primary author of a U.S. Pharmaceutical Patent.

Vahe is married to Marie (Hosepian) who holds Doctor in Nursing Practitioner degree and is a former Lieutenant Colonel with the U.S. Army Reserves. They are blessed with two grown up sons.

Authors' email addresses:

vapelian@yahoo.com

vapelian@gmail.com

Made in the USA
Charleston, SC
13 September 2015